Disney® Songs

The following songs are the property of:

Bourne Co.
Music Publishers
5 West 37th Street
New York, NY 10018

BABY MINE
GIVE A LITTLE WHISTLE
HEIGH-HO
SOME DAY MY PRINCE WILL COME
WHEN YOU WISH UPON A STAR
WHISTLE WHILE YOU WORK
WHO'S AFRAID OF THE BIG BAD WOLF?

ISBN 978-1-61780-374-1

Walt Disney Music Company
Wonderland Music Company, Inc.

DISTRIBUTED BY

HAL•LEONARD®
CORPORATION

7777 W. BLUEMOUND RD. P.O. BOX 13819 MILWAUKEE, WI 53213

Visit Hal Leonard Online at
www.halleonard.com

Alice in Wonderland

from Walt Disney's ALICE IN WONDERLAND

Words by Bob Hilliard
Music by Sammy Fain

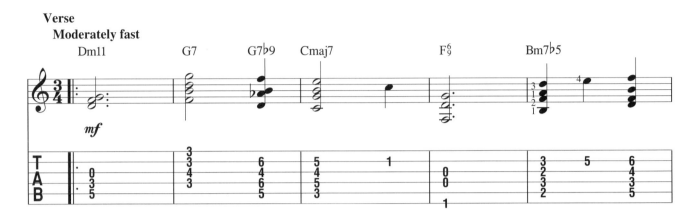

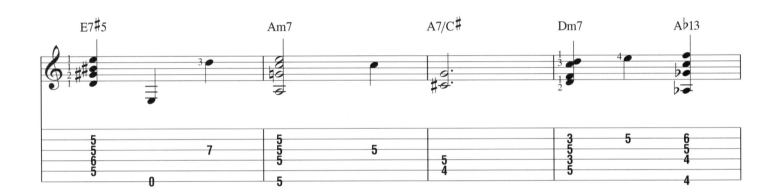

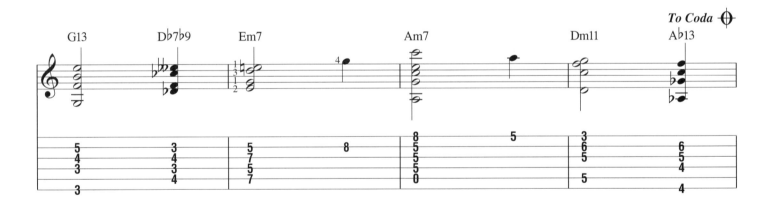

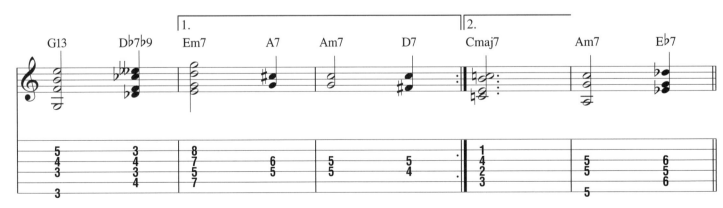

Bridge

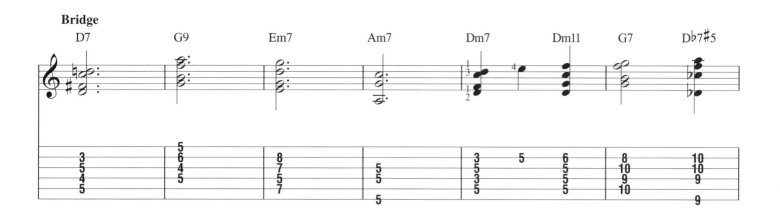

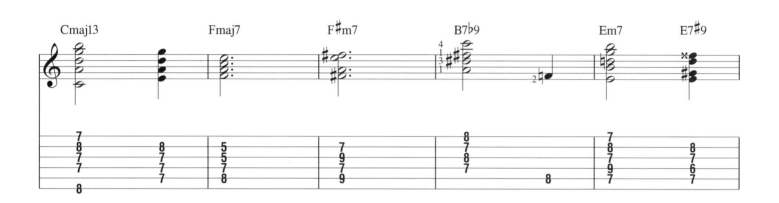

D.C. al Coda

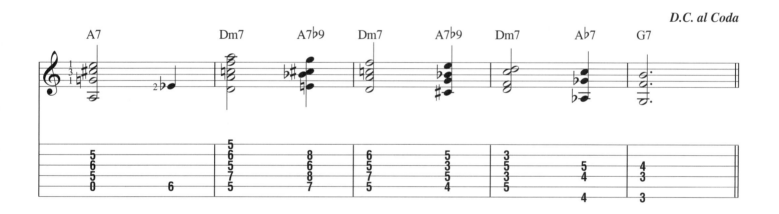

Coda

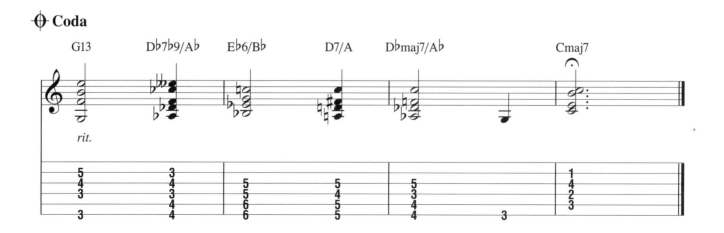

Baby Mine

from Walt Disney's DUMBO

Words by Ned Washington
Music by Frank Churchill

Verse
Moderately slow

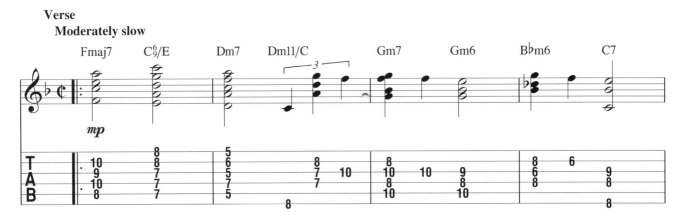

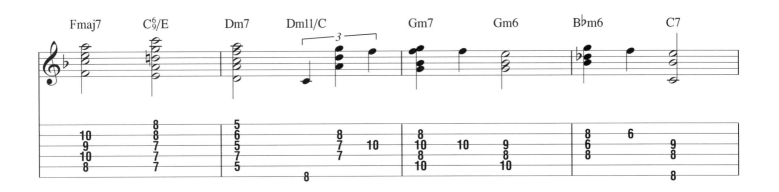

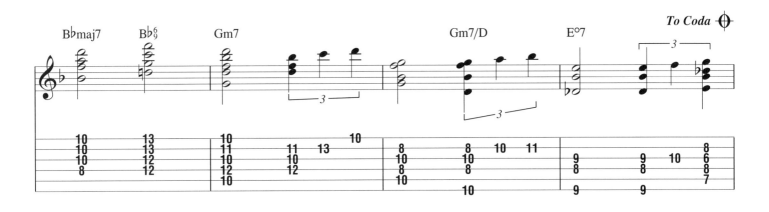

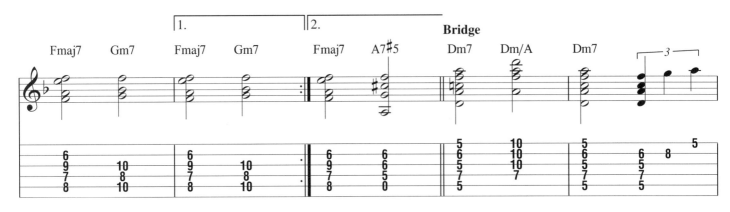

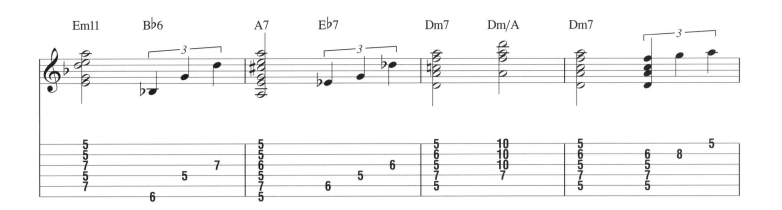

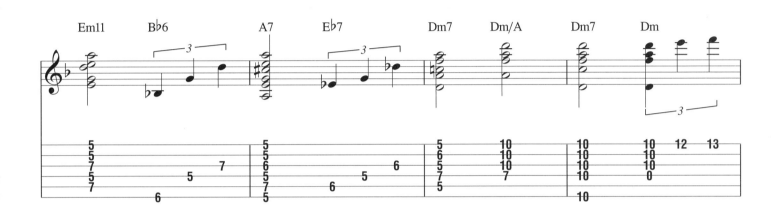

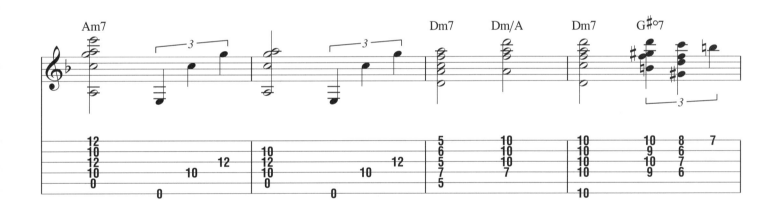

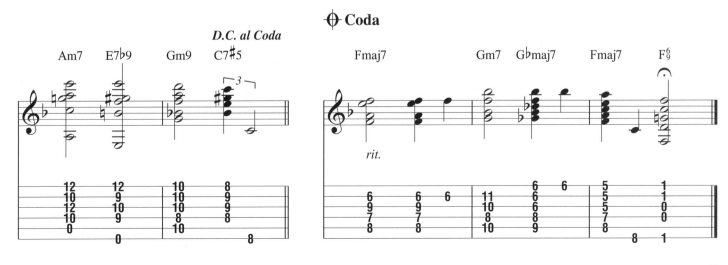

Bibbidi-Bobbidi-Boo
(The Magic Song)
from Walt Disney's CINDERELLA

Words by Jerry Livingston
Music by Mack David and Al Hoffman

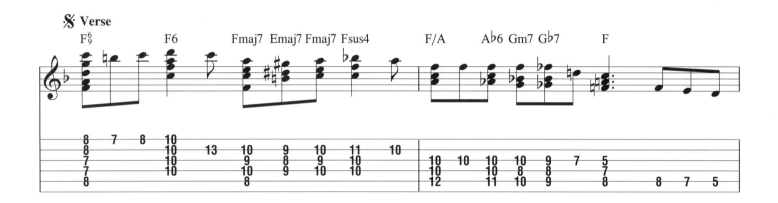

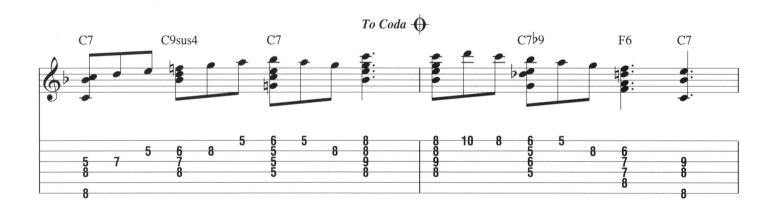

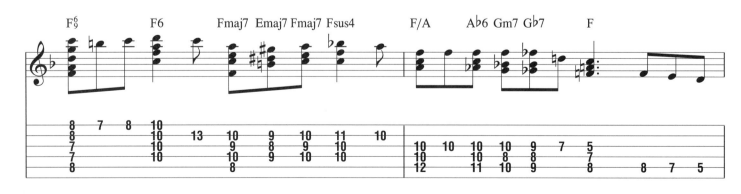

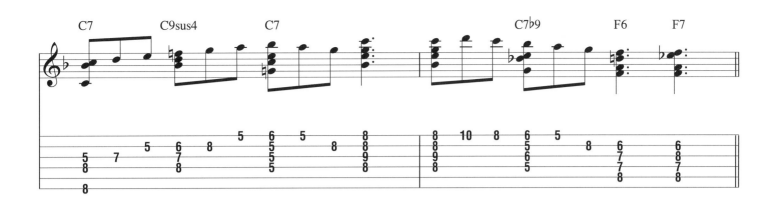

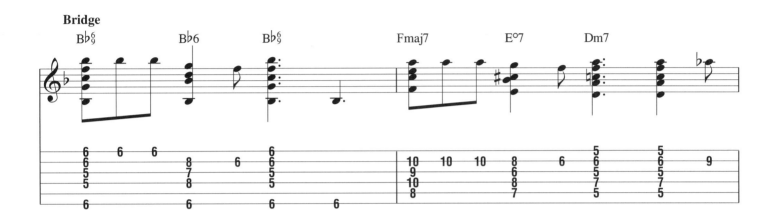

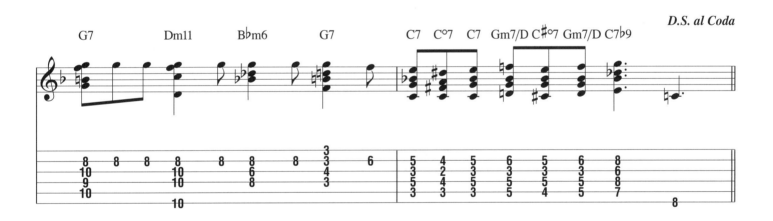

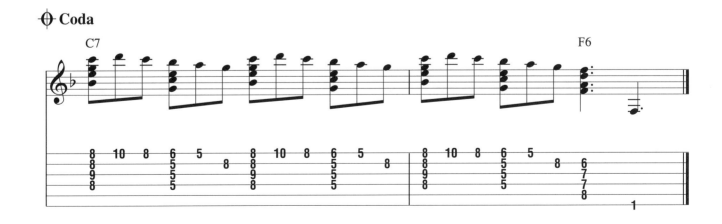

Can You Feel the Love Tonight

from Walt Disney Pictures' THE LION KING

Music by Elton John
Lyrics by Tim Rice

Intro
Moderately slow

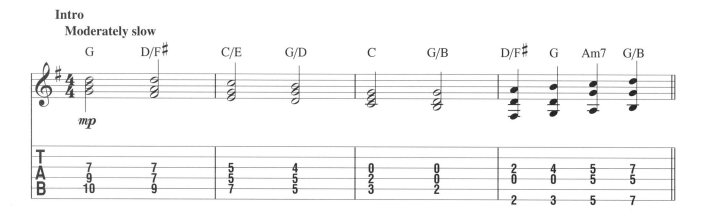

Verse

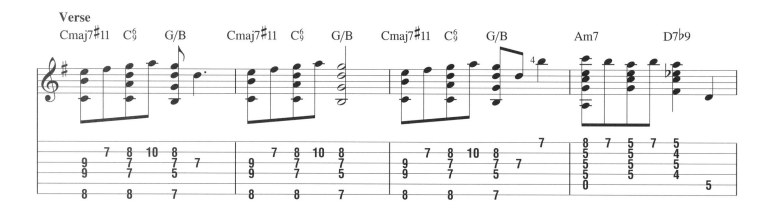

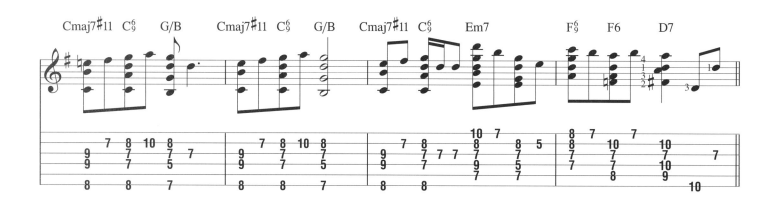

Chorus

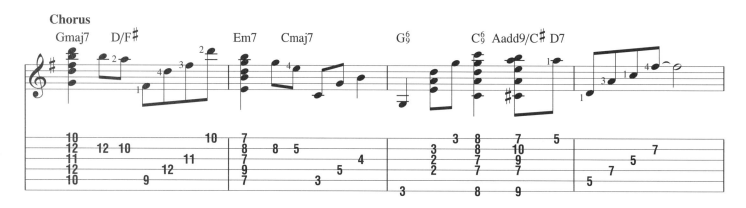

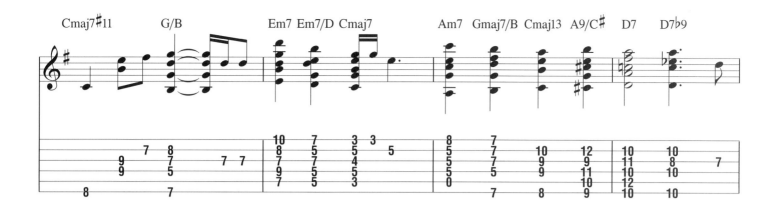

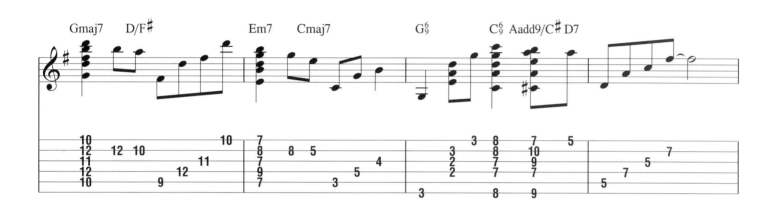

To Coda ⊕

D.C. al Coda

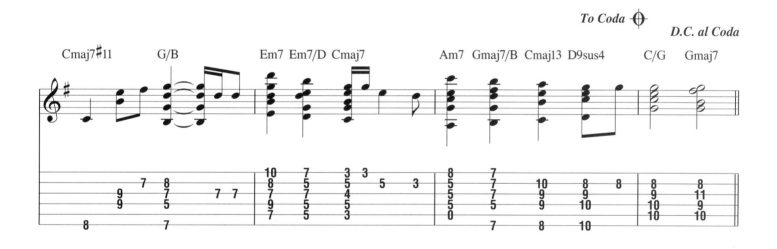

⊕ **Coda**

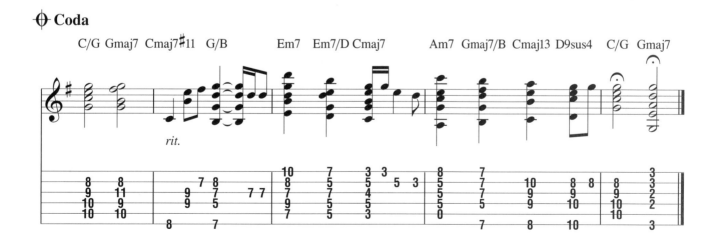

Candle on the Water

from Walt Disney's PETE'S DRAGON

Words and Music by Al Kasha and Joel Hirschhorn

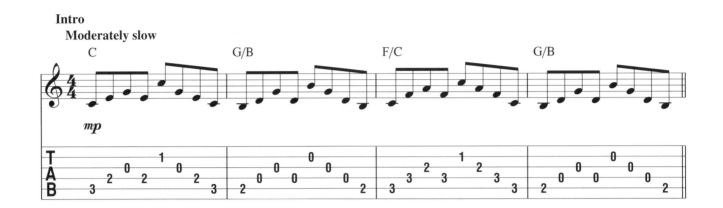

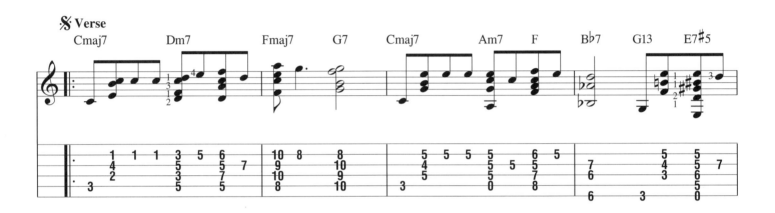

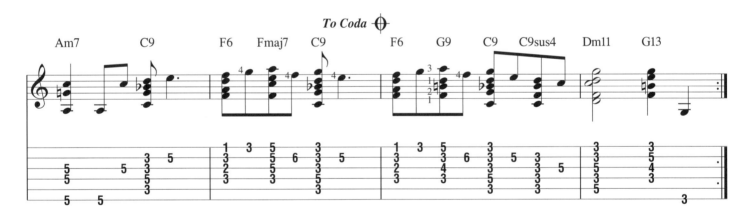

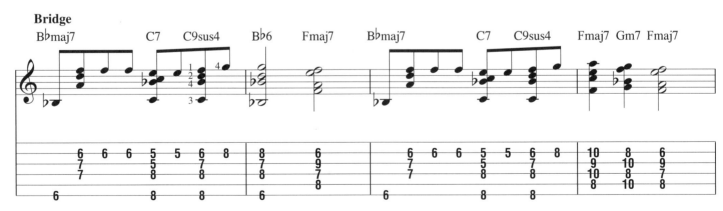

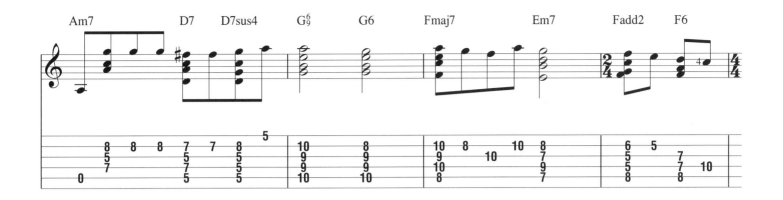

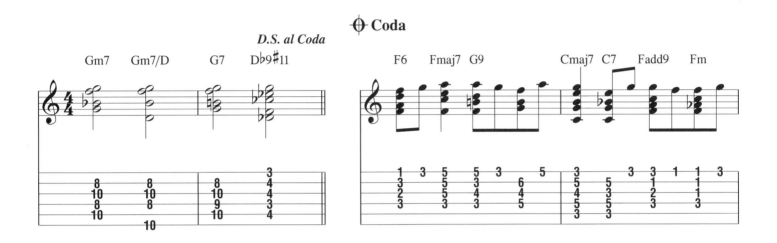

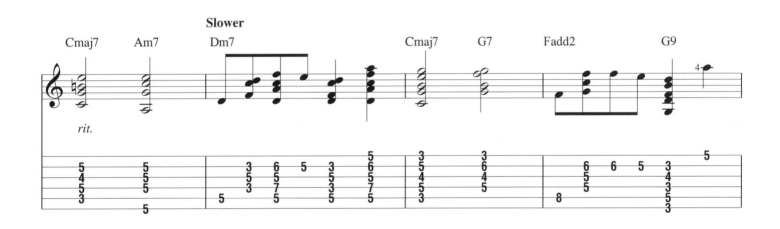

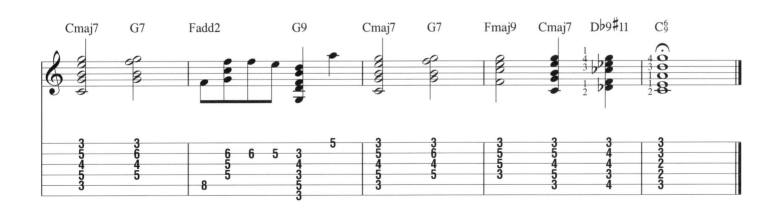

Beauty and the Beast

from Walt Disney's BEAUTY AND THE BEAST

Lyrics by Howard Ashman
Music by Alan Menken

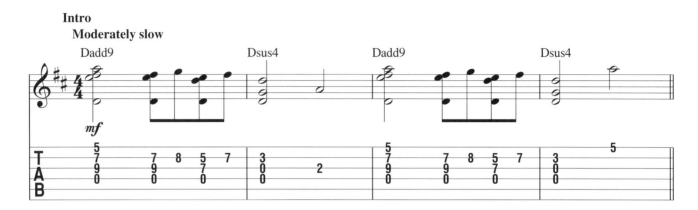

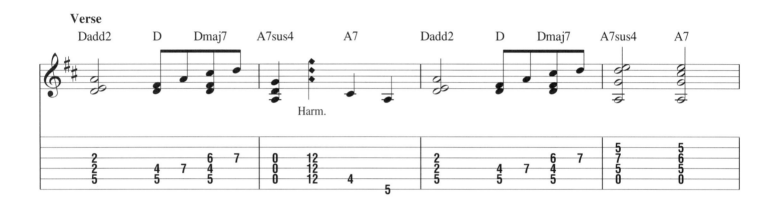

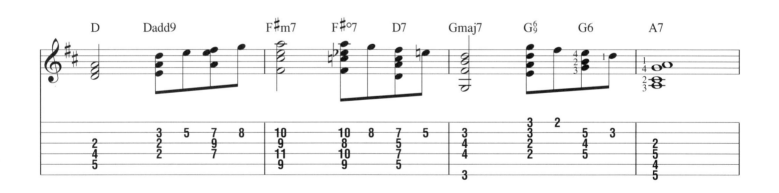

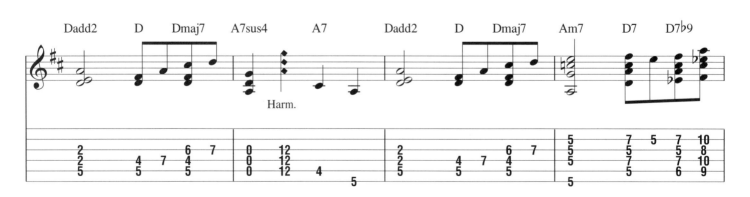

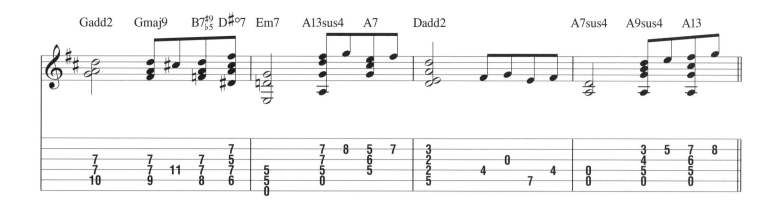

Bridge

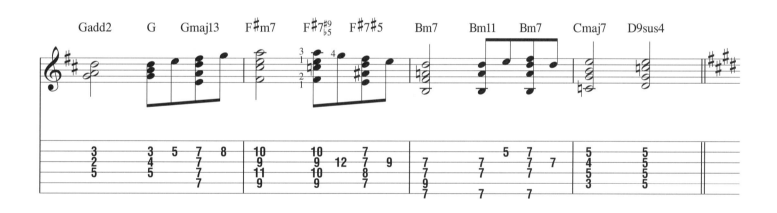

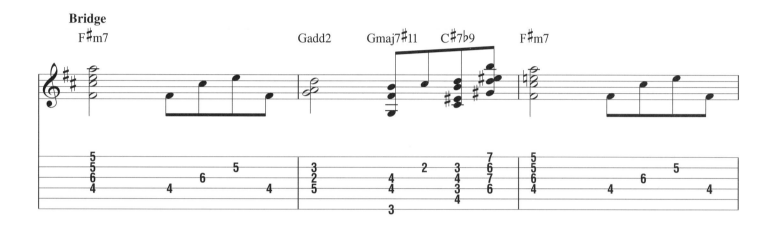

Verse

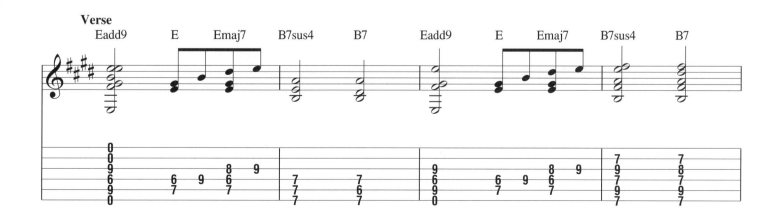

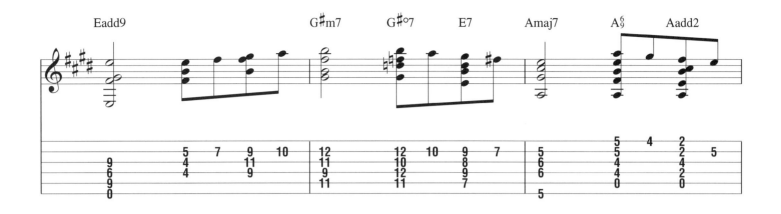

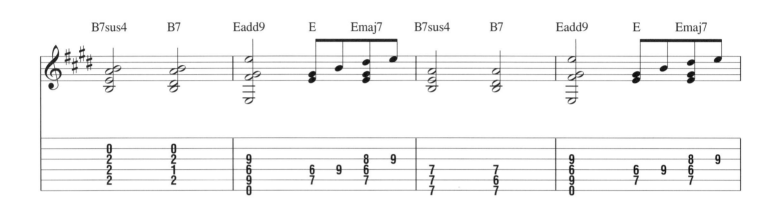

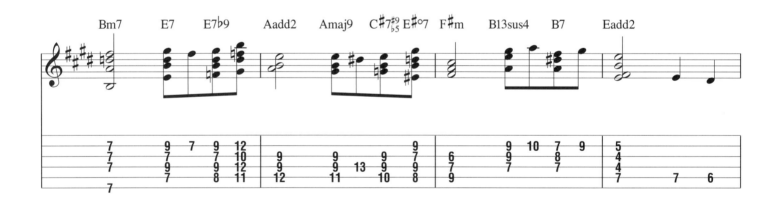

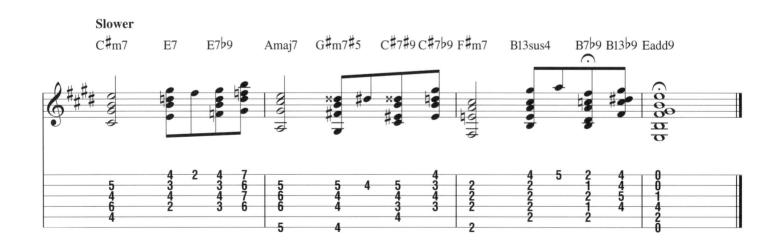

Chim Chim Cher-ee

from Walt Disney's MARY POPPINS

Words and Music by Richard M. Sherman and Robert B. Sherman

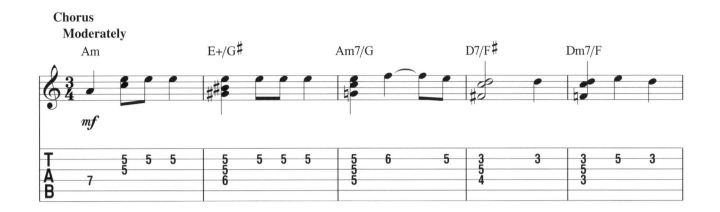

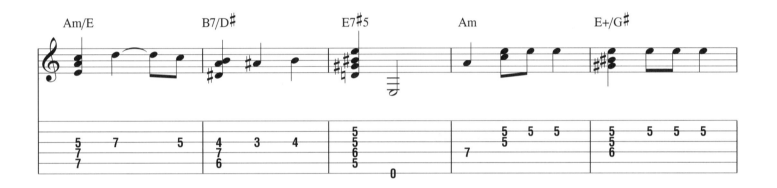

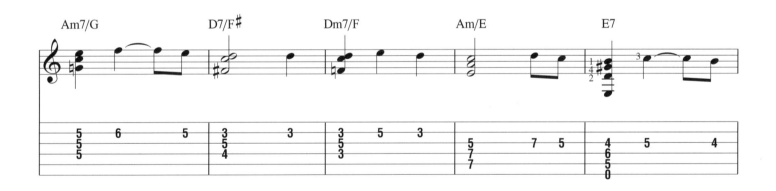

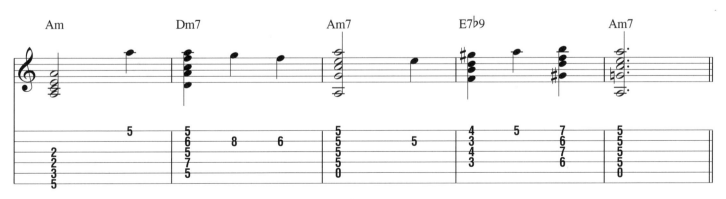

Verse

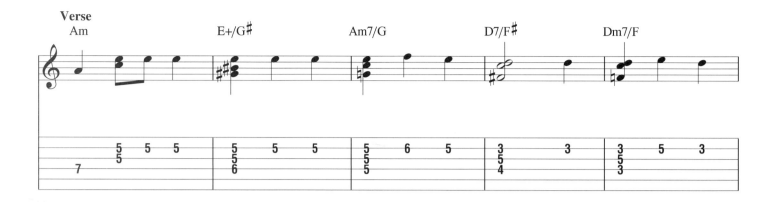

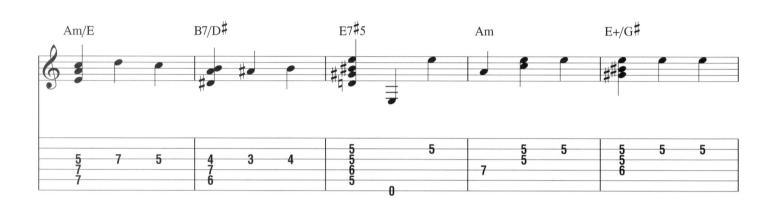

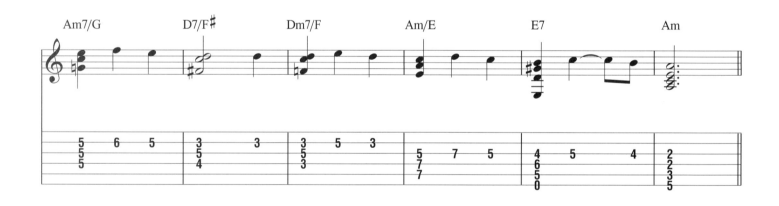

Chorus

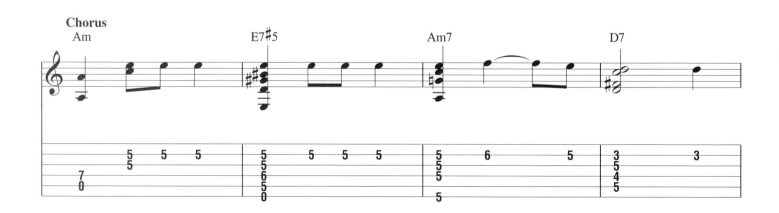

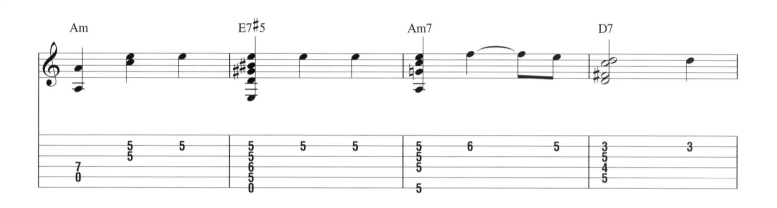

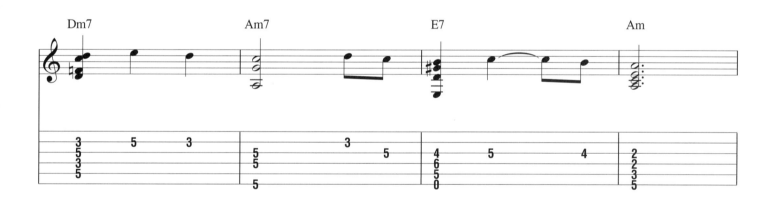

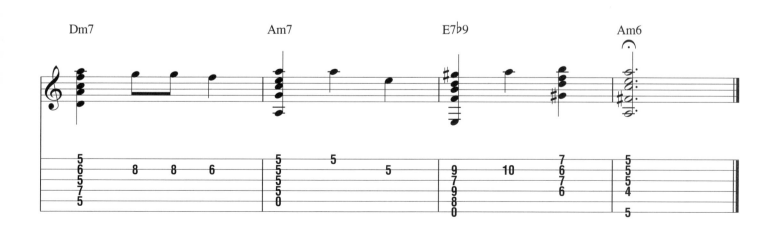

Circle of Life
from Walt Disney Pictures' THE LION KING

Music by Elton John
Lyrics by Tim Rice

Intro
Moderately

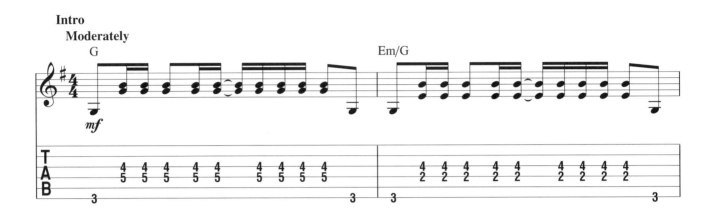

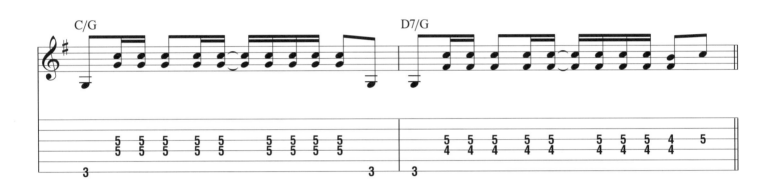

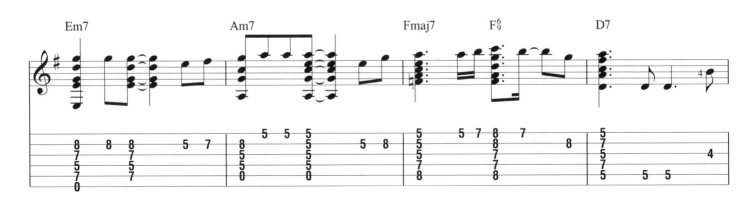

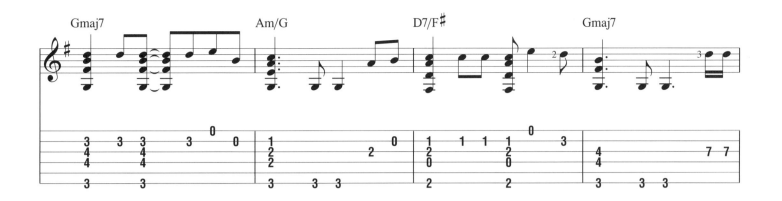

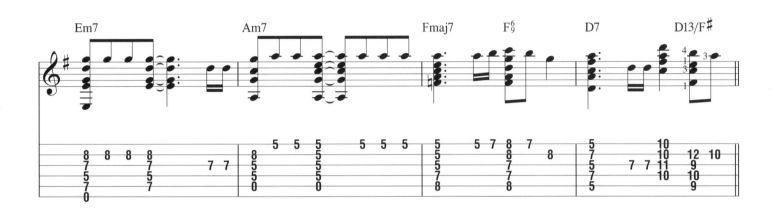

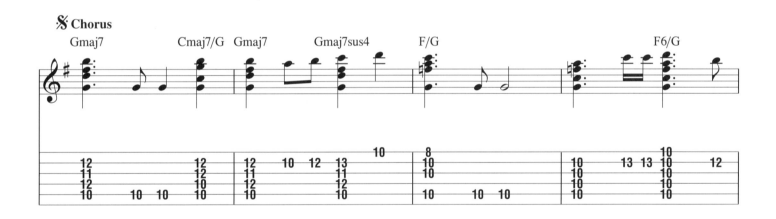

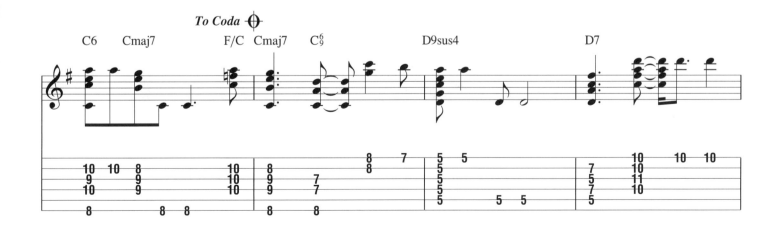

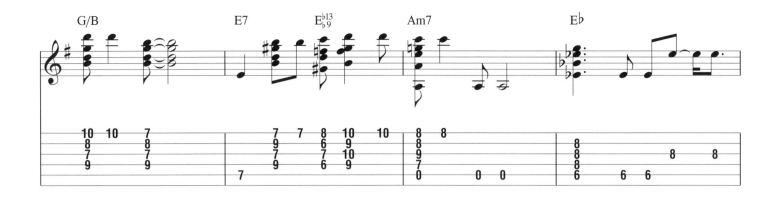

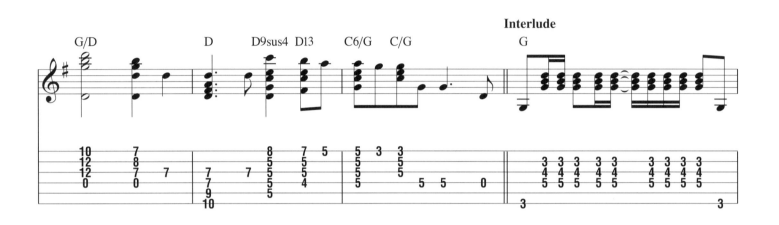

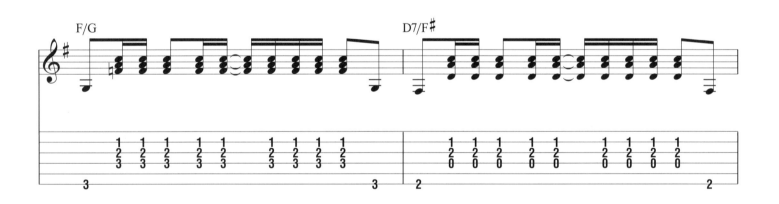

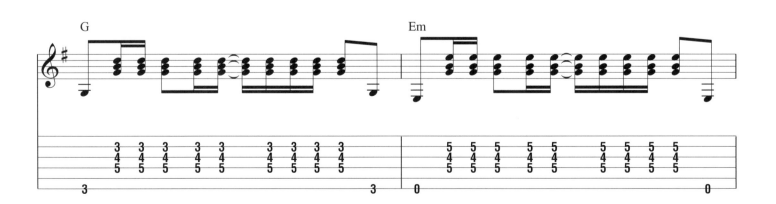

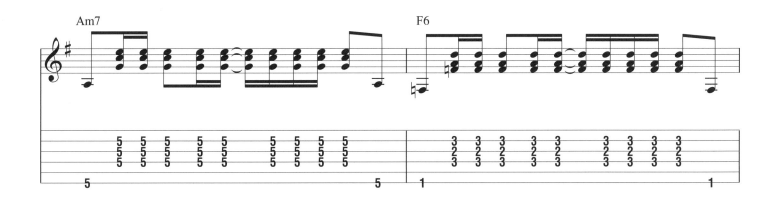

⊕ Coda

D.S. al Coda

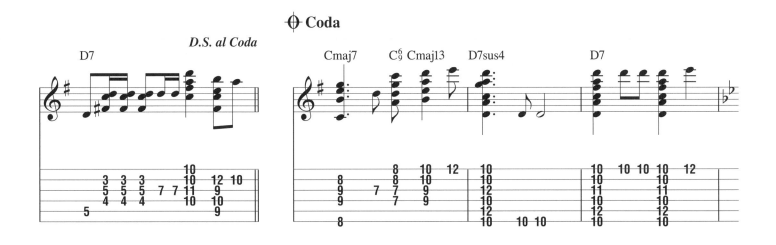

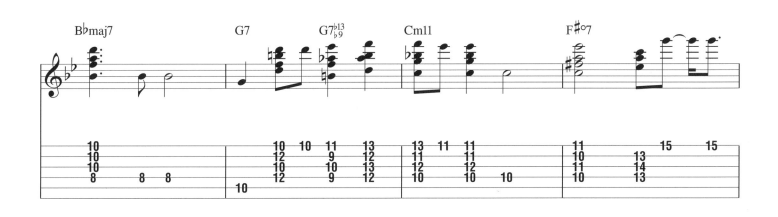

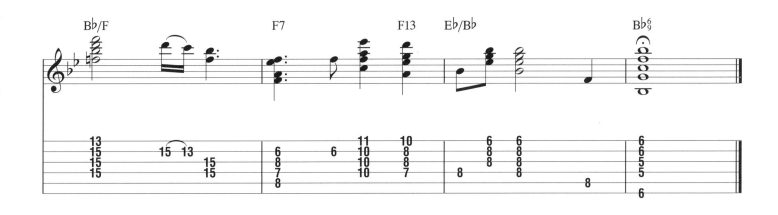

Colors of the Wind

from Walt Disney's POCAHONTAS

Music by Alan Menken
Lyrics by Stephen Schwartz

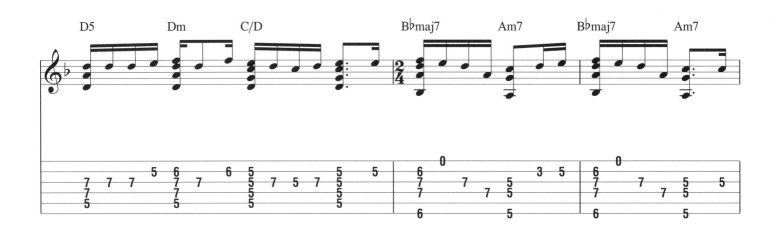

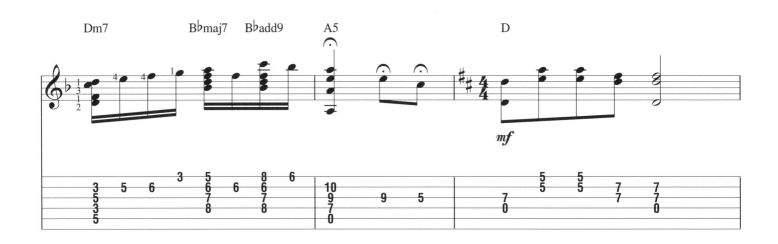

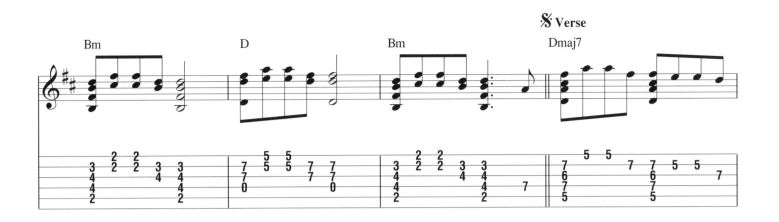

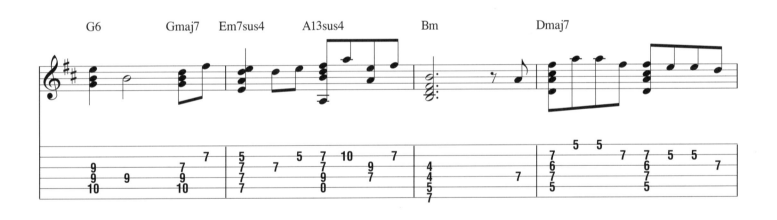

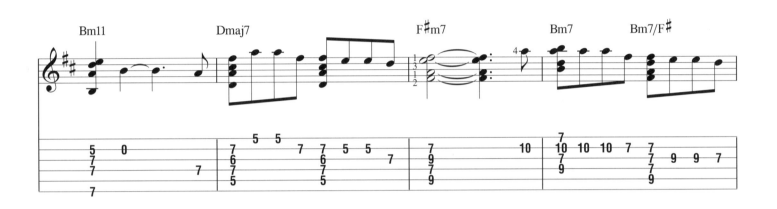

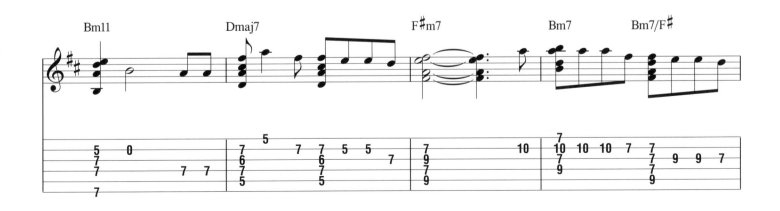

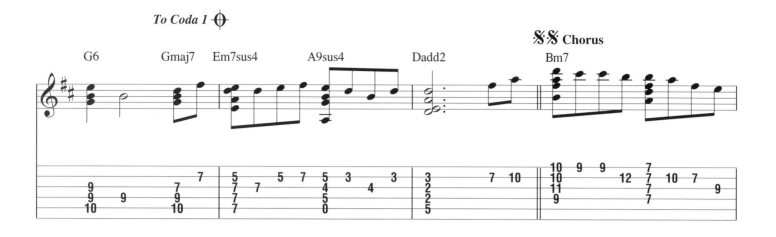

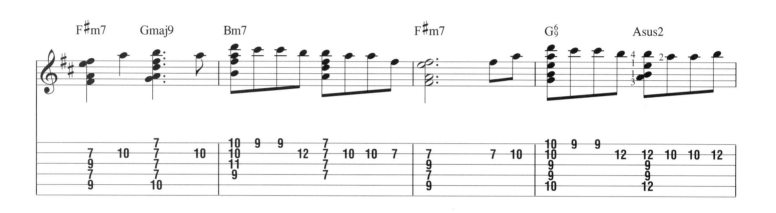

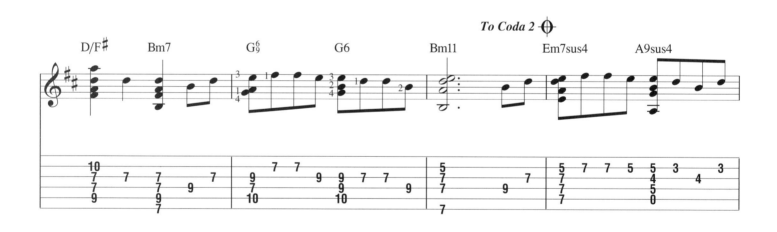

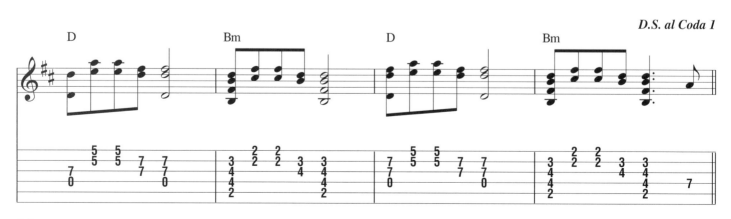

Coda 1

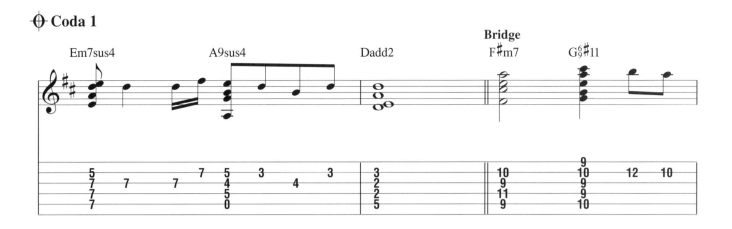

D.S.S. al Coda 2

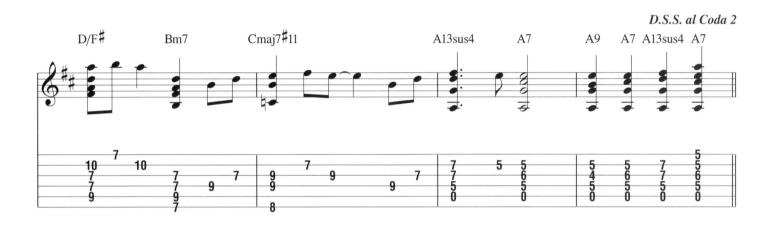

Coda 2

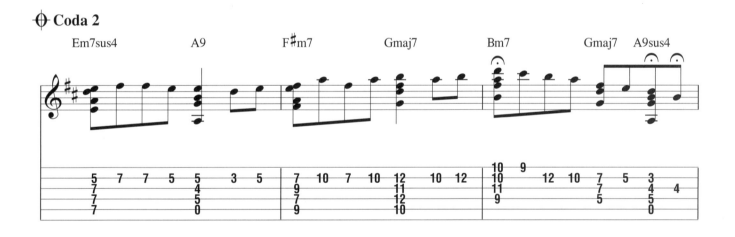

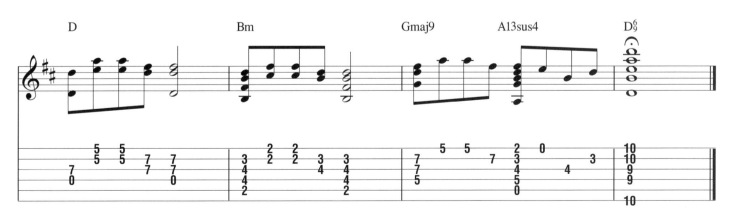

Cruella de Vil

from Walt Disney's 101 DALMATIANS

Words and Music by Mel Leven

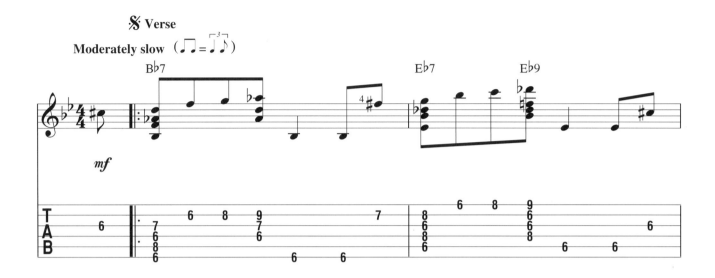

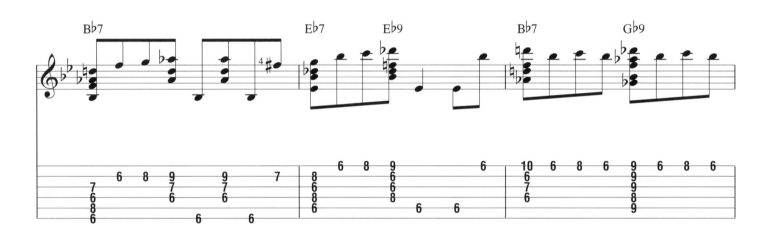

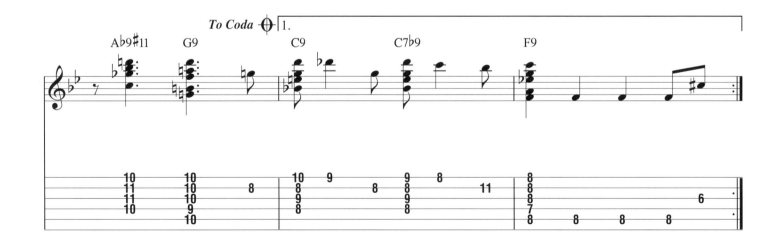

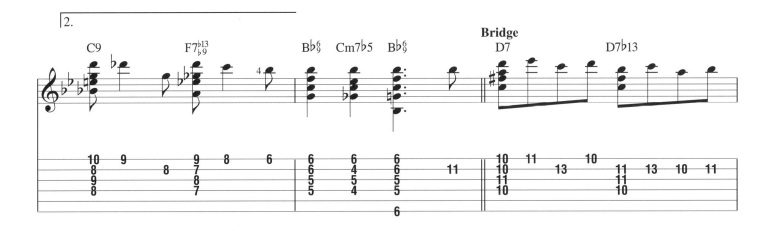

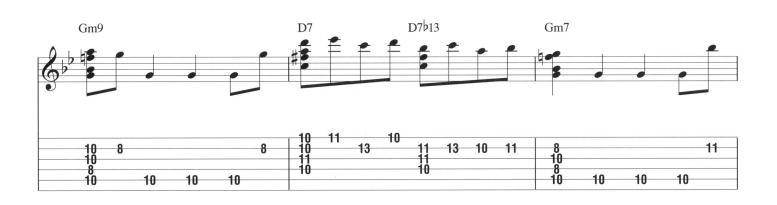

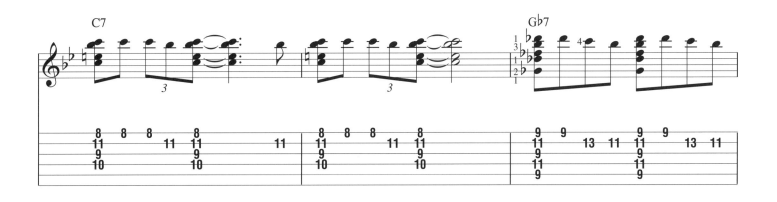

⊕ Coda

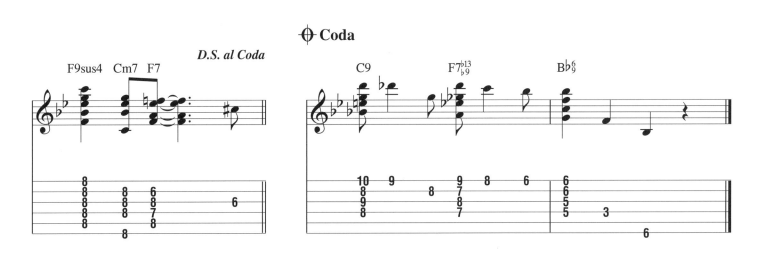

A Dream Is a Wish Your Heart Makes

from Walt Disney's CINDERELLA

Words and Music by Mack David, Al Hoffman and Jerry Livingston

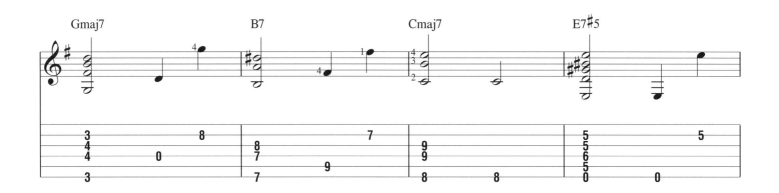

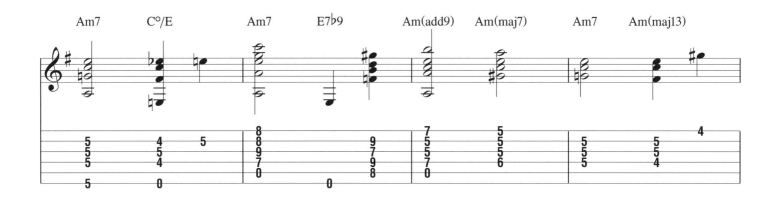

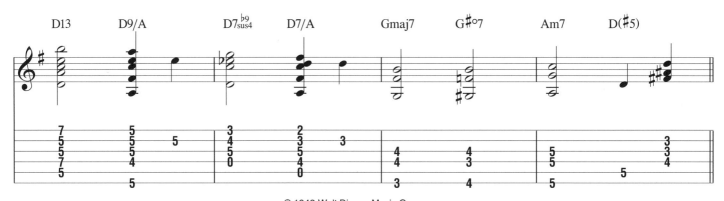

Outro

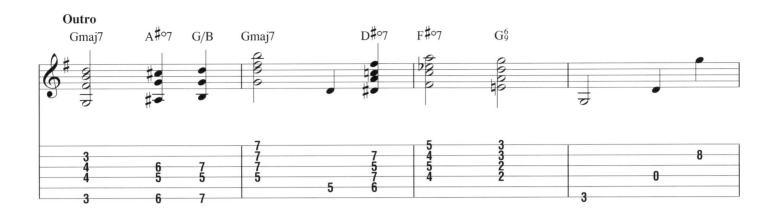

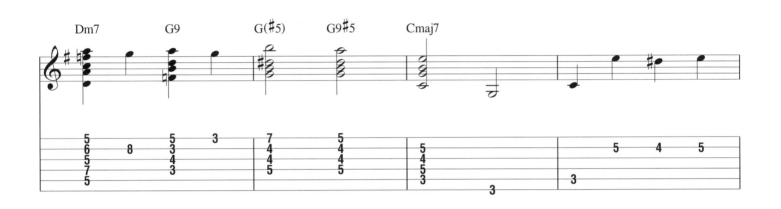

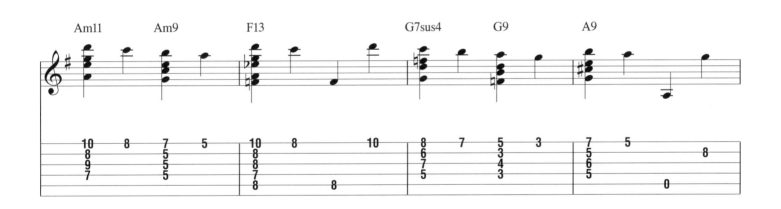

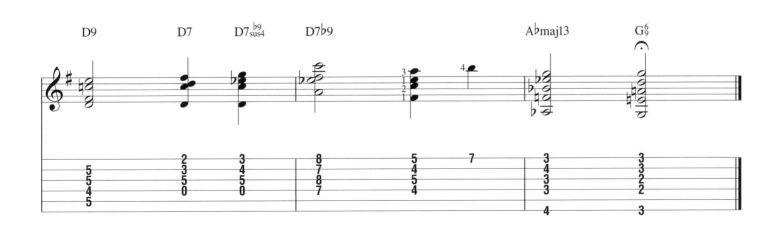

Give a Little Whistle

from Walt Disney's PINOCCHIO

Words by Ned Washington
Music by Leigh Harline

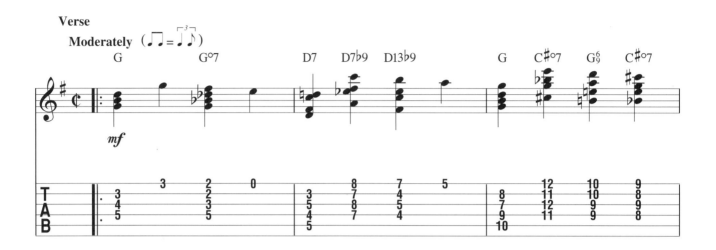

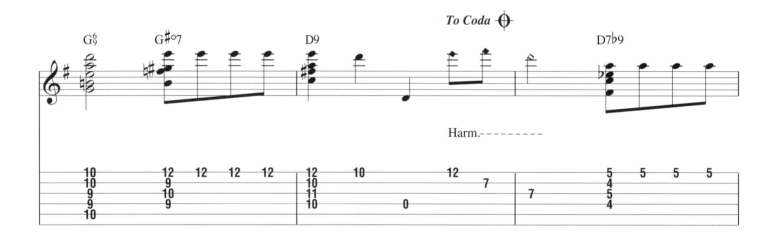

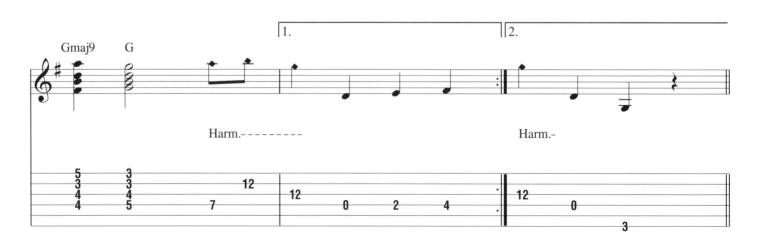

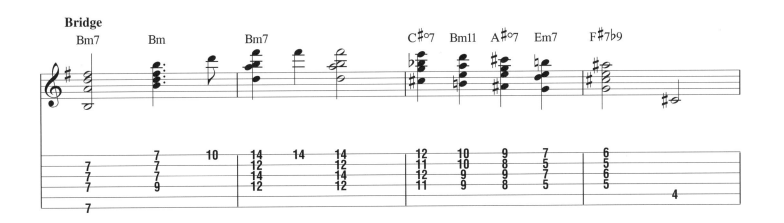

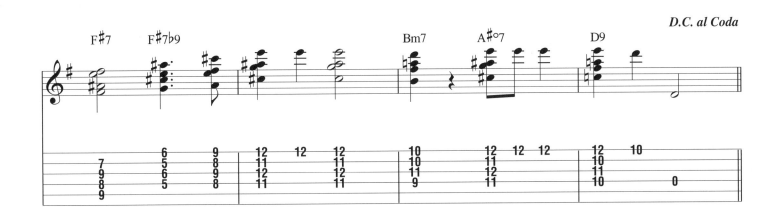

D.C. al Coda

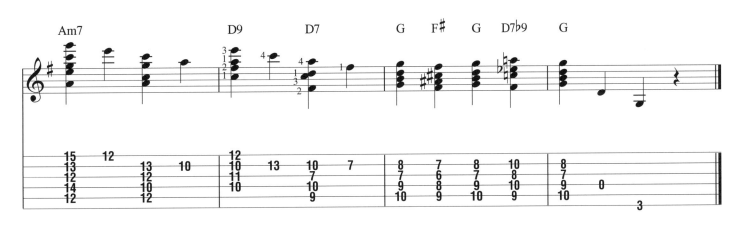

He's a Tramp

from Walt Disney's LADY AND THE TRAMP

Words and Music by Peggy Lee and Sonny Burke

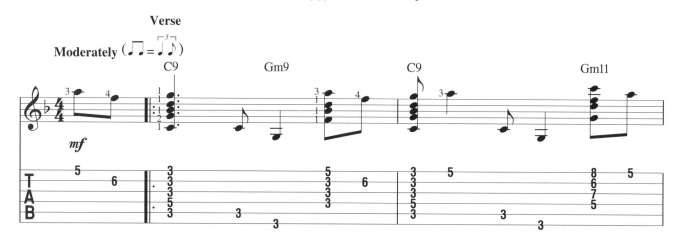

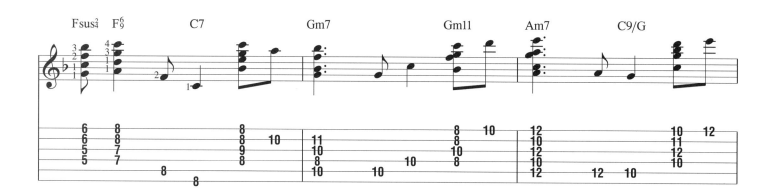

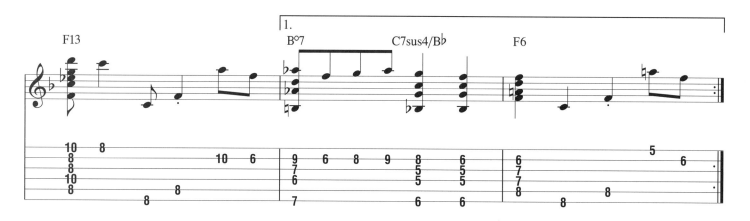

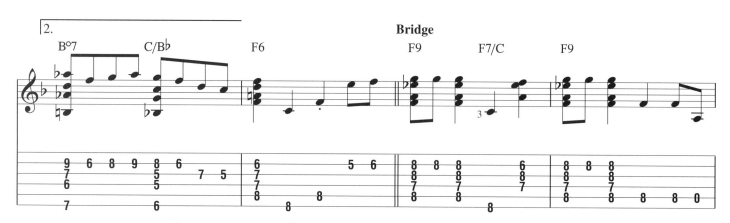

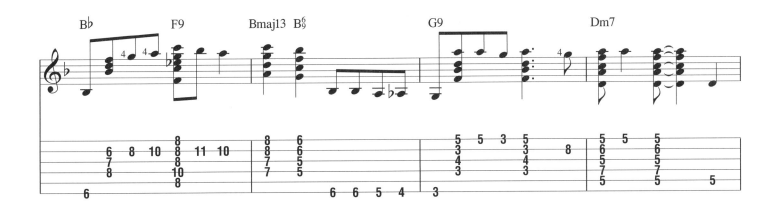

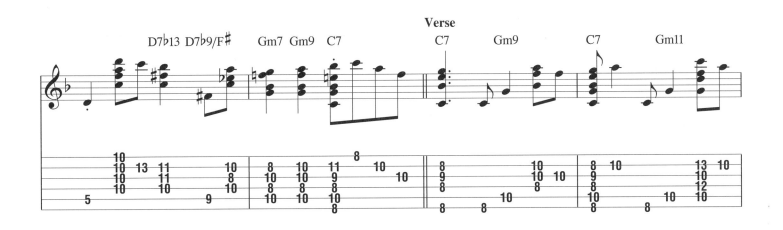

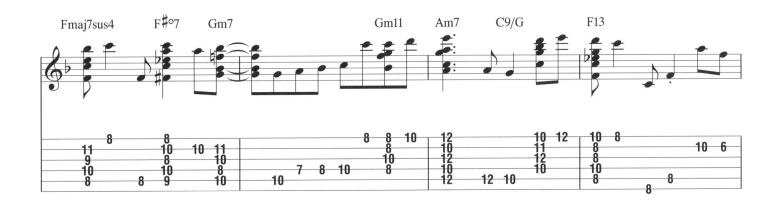

Heigh-Ho

The Dwarfs' Marching Song from Walt Disney's SNOW WHITE AND THE SEVEN DWARFS

Words by Larry Morey
Music by Frank Churchill

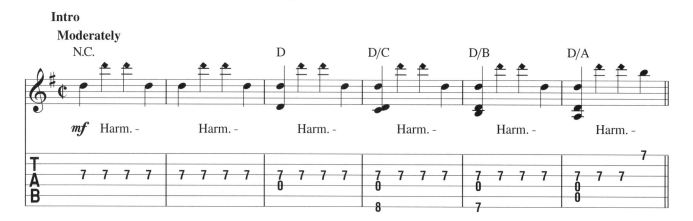

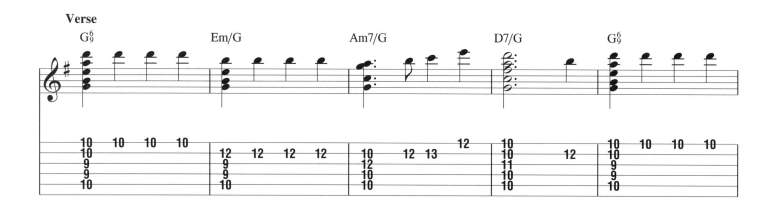

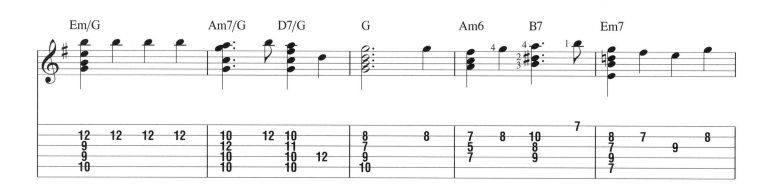

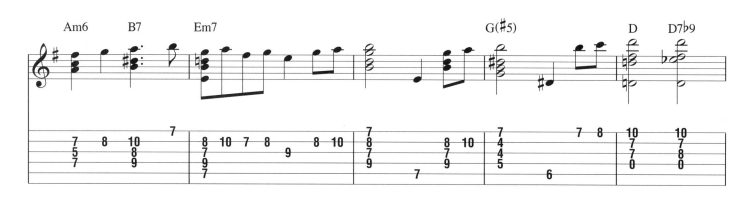

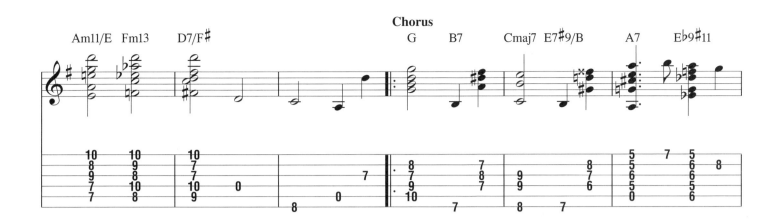

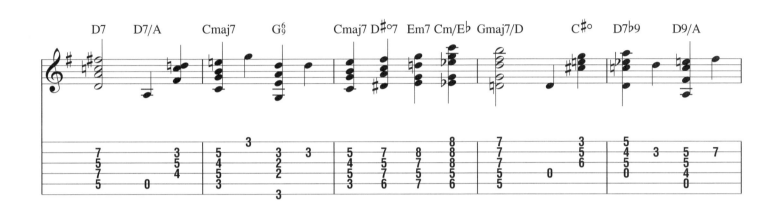

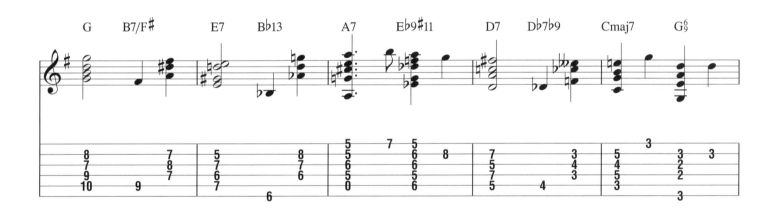

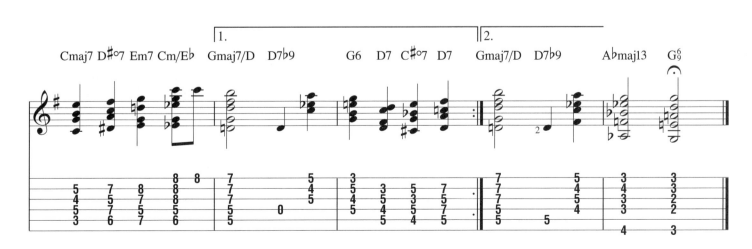

If I Never Knew You
(Love Theme from POCAHONTAS)
from Walt Disney's POCAHONTAS

Music by Alan Menken
Lyrics by Stephen Schwartz

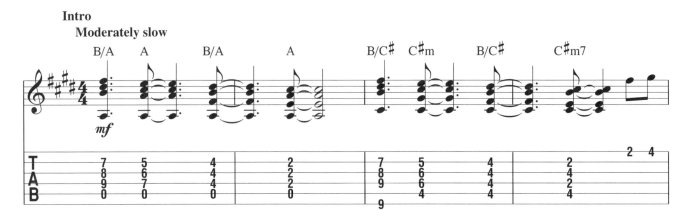

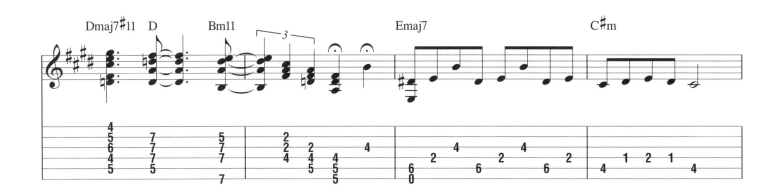

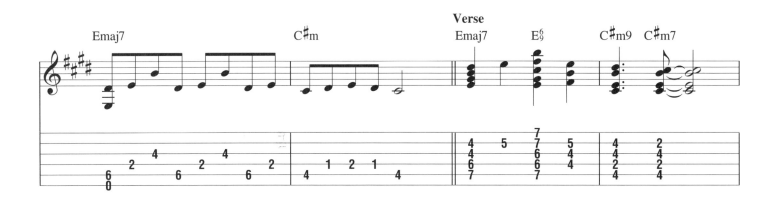

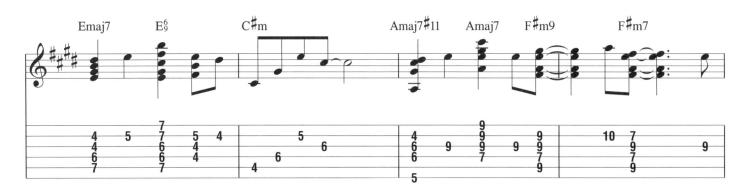

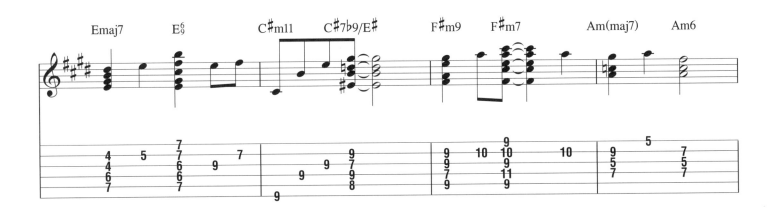

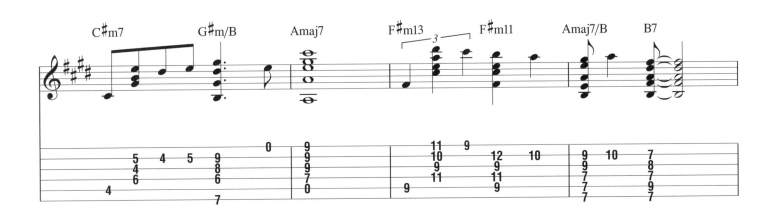

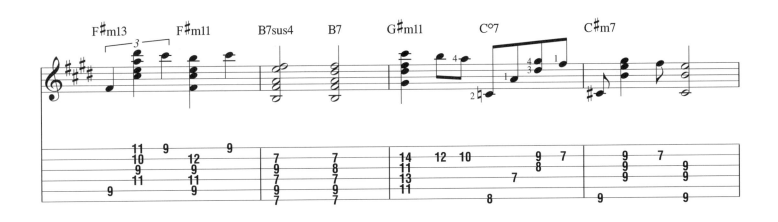

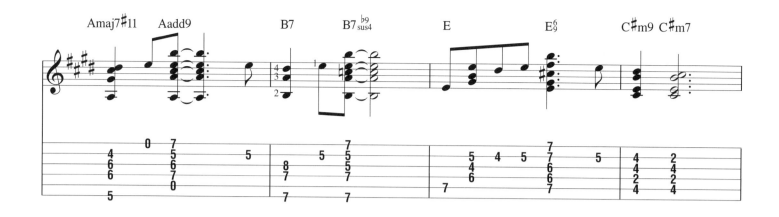

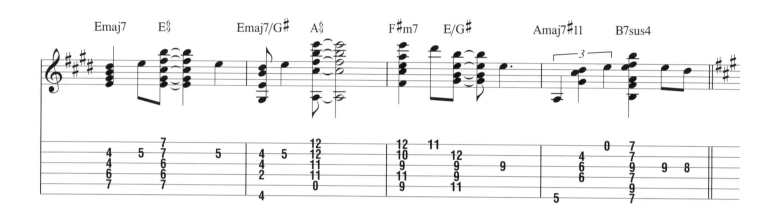

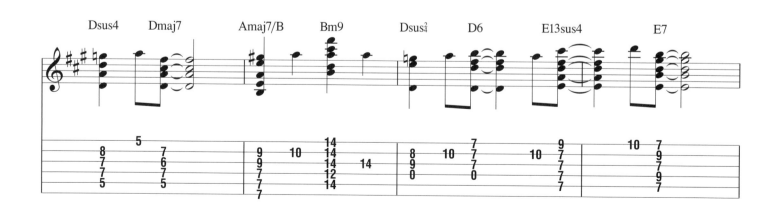

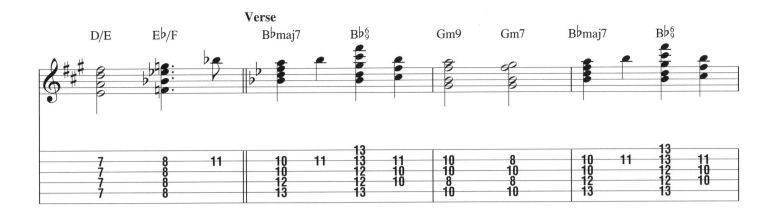

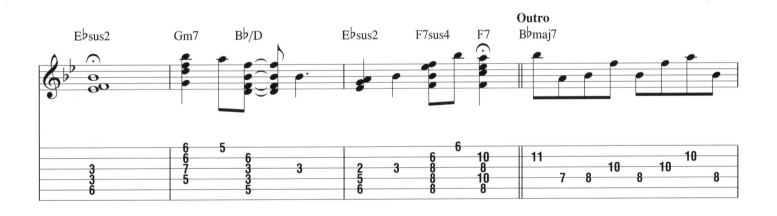

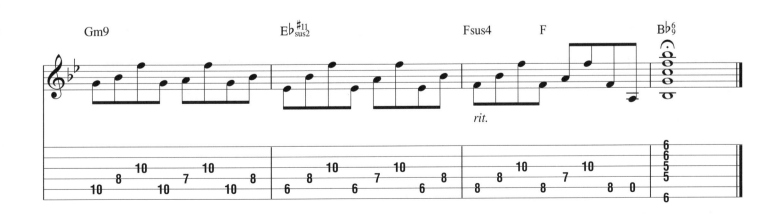

Once Upon a Dream

from Walt Disney's SLEEPING BEAUTY

Words and Music by Sammy Fain and Jack Lawrence
Adapted from a Theme by Tchaikovsky

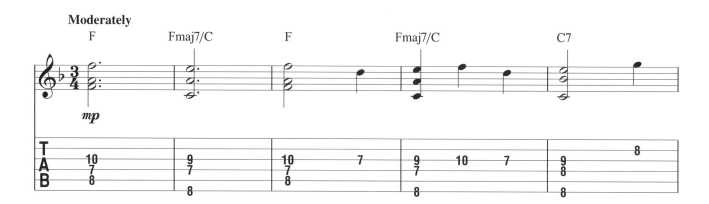

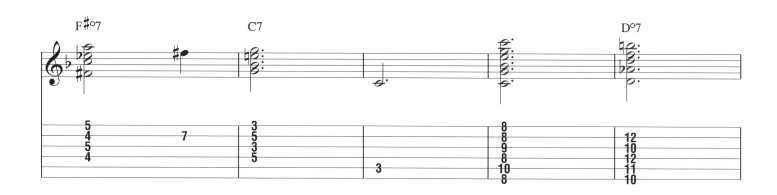

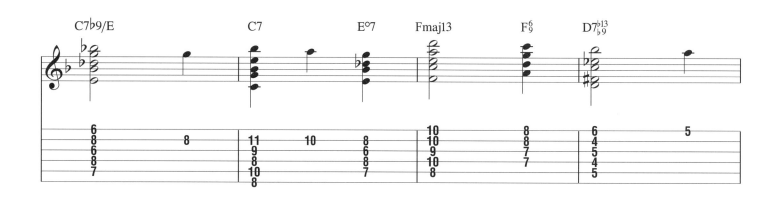

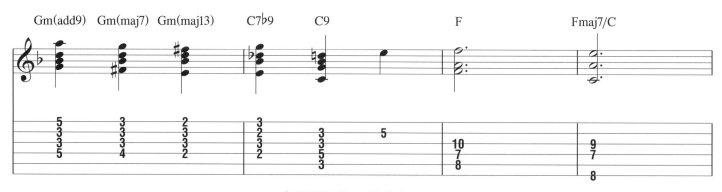

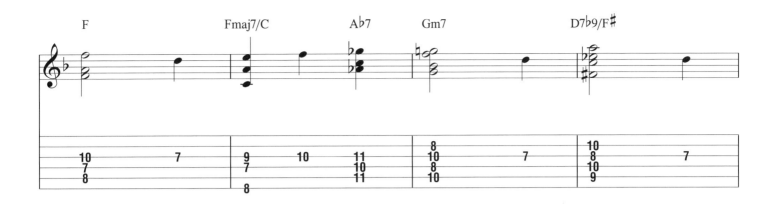

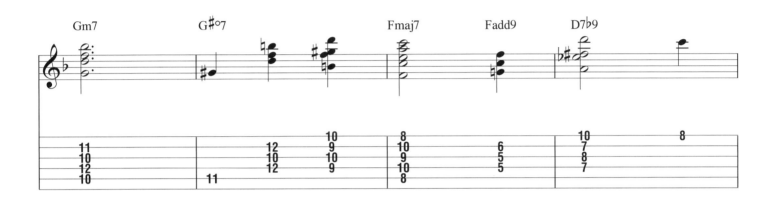

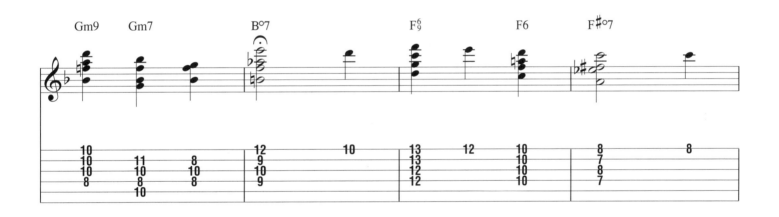

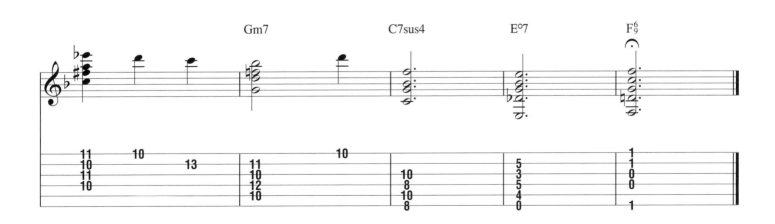

Some Day My Prince Will Come

from Walt Disney's SNOW WHITE AND THE SEVEN DWARFS

Words by Larry Morey
Music by Frank Churchill

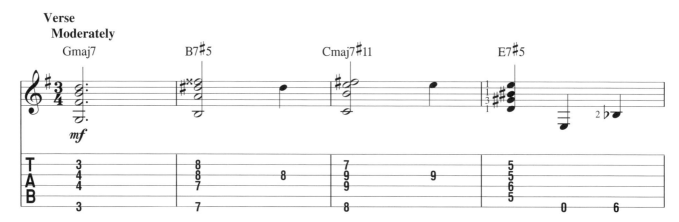

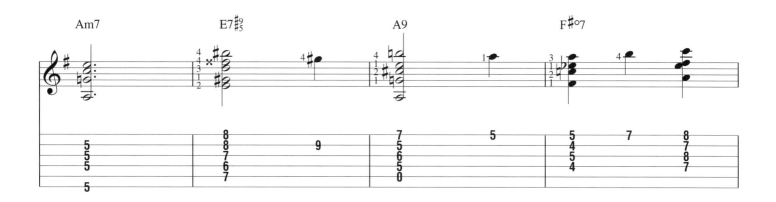

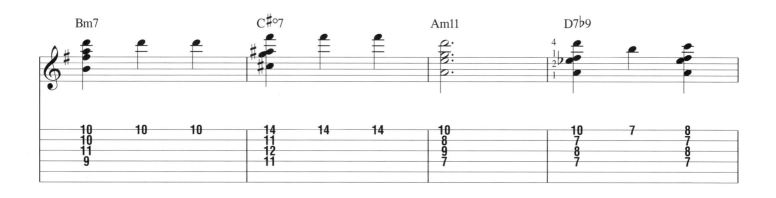

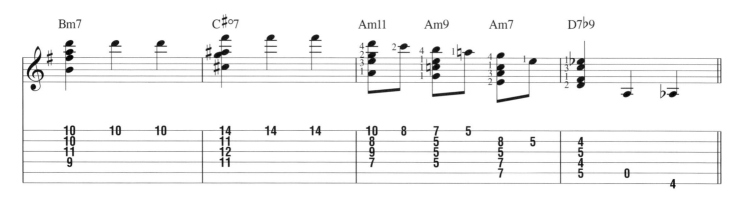

Verse

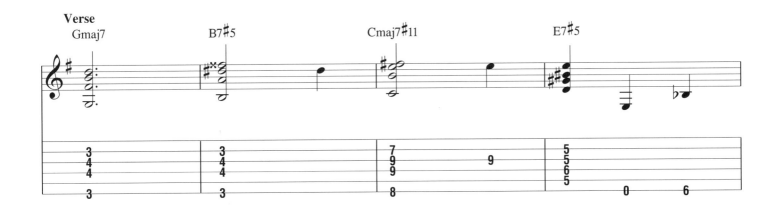

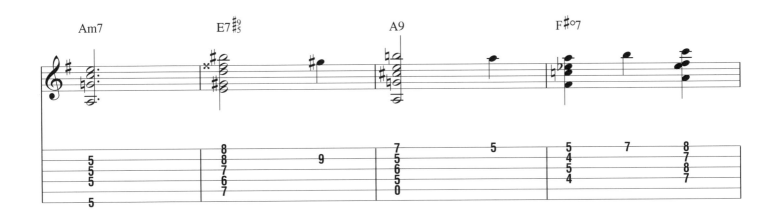

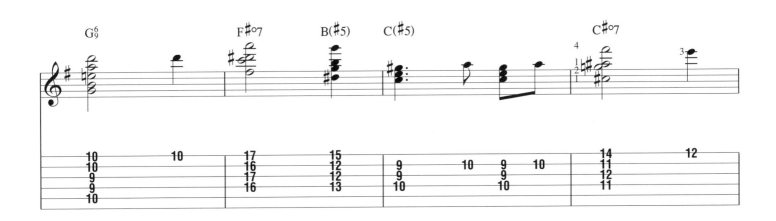

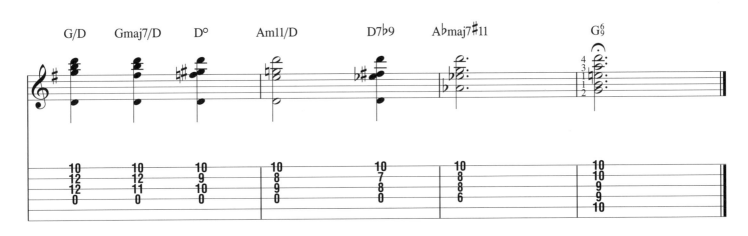

Mickey Mouse March

from Walt Disney's THE MICKEY MOUSE CLUB

Words and Music by Jimmie Dodd

Supercalifragilisticexpialidocious

from Walt Disney's MARY POPPINS

Words and Music by Richard M. Sherman and Robert B. Sherman

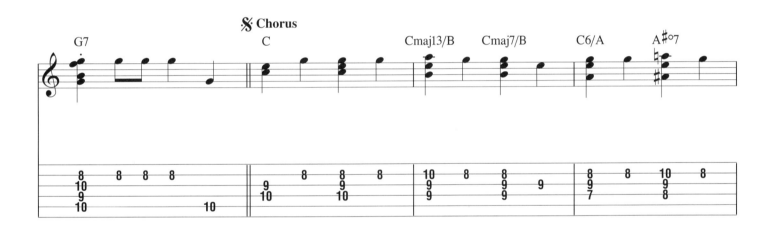

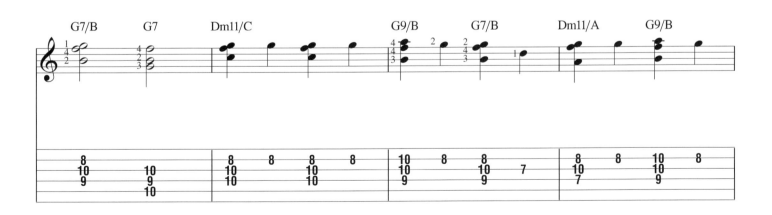

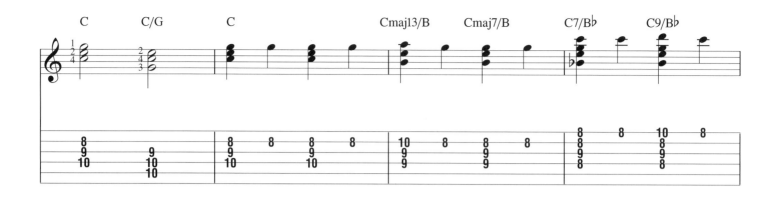

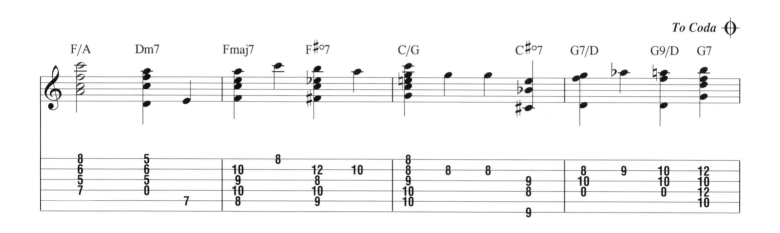

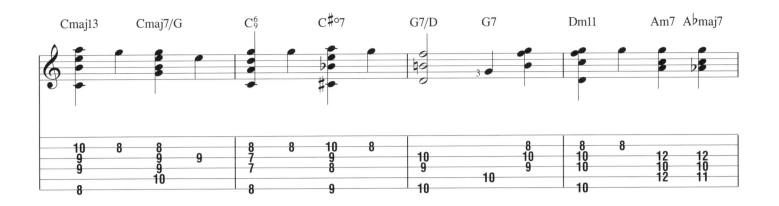

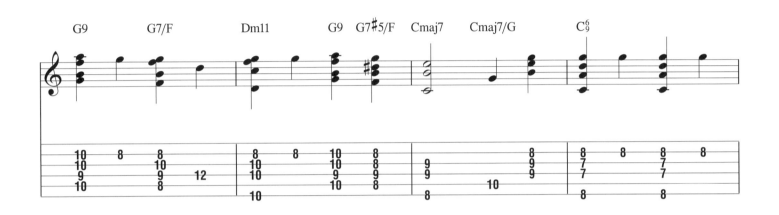

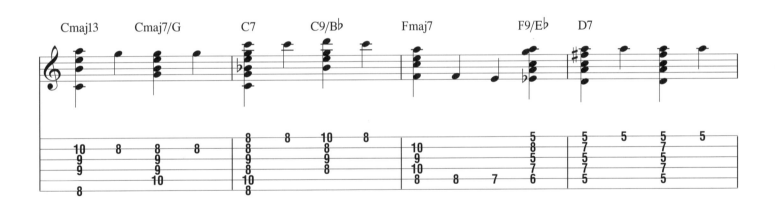

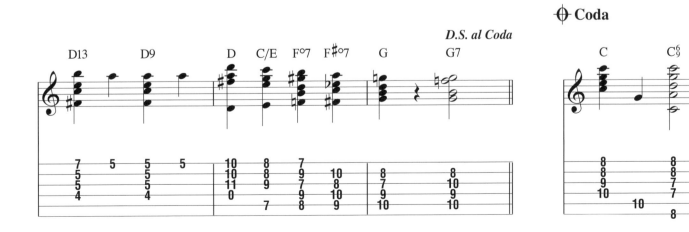

Under the Sea
from Walt Disney's THE LITTLE MERMAID

Music by Alan Menken
Lyrics by Howard Ashman

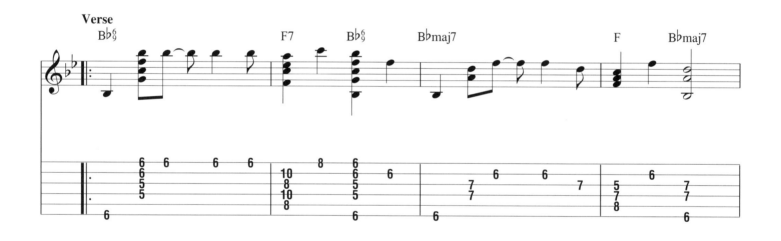

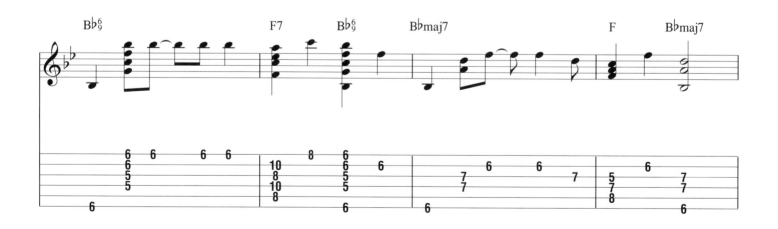

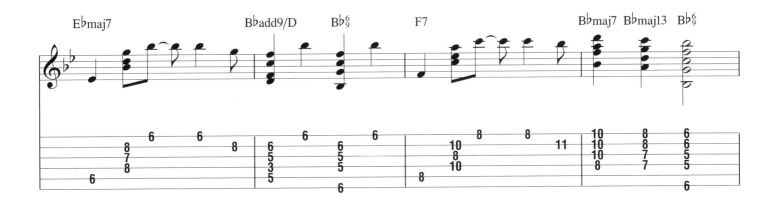

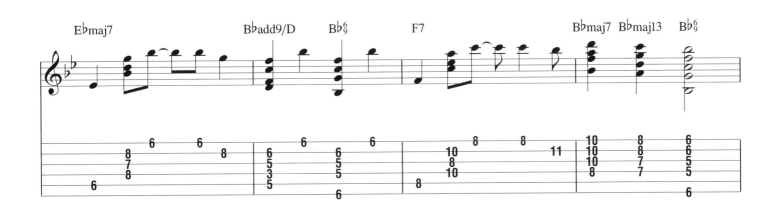

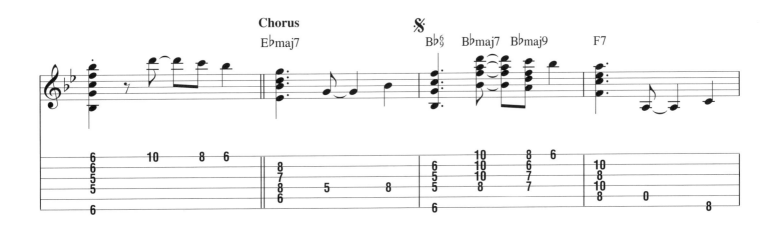

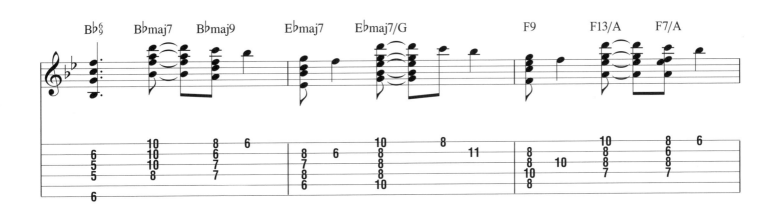

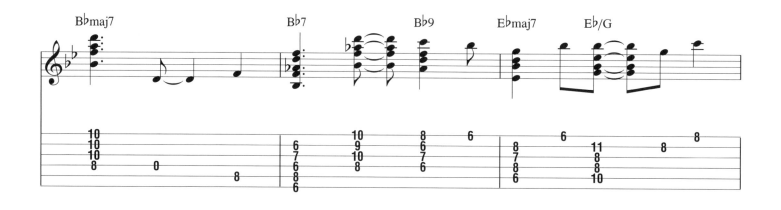

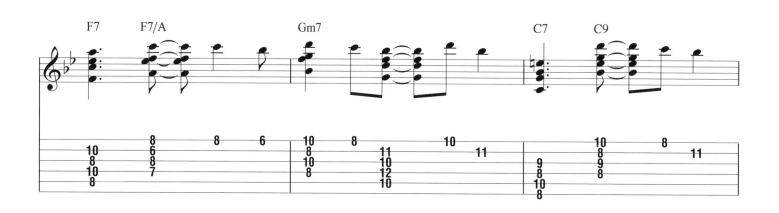

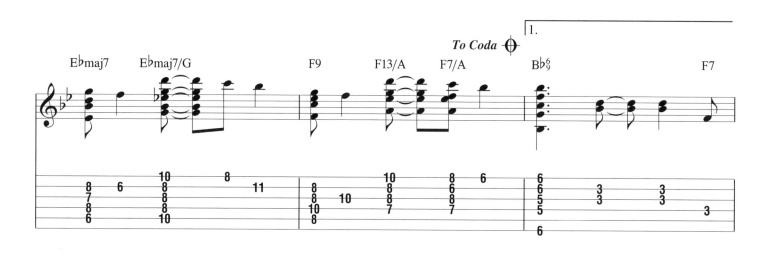

⊕ Coda

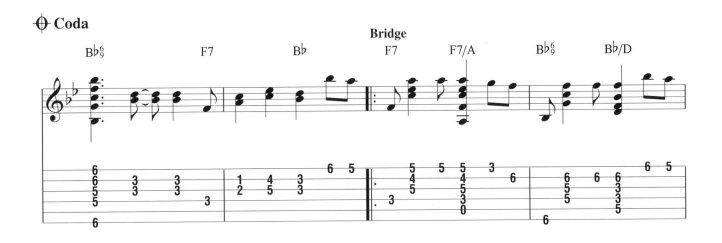

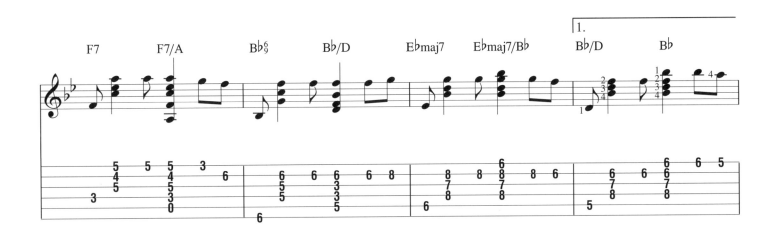

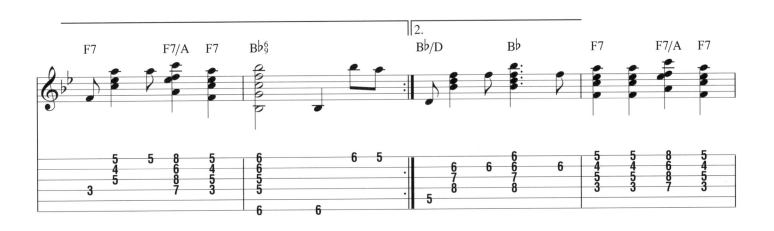

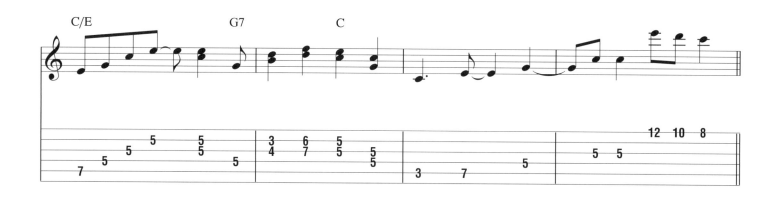

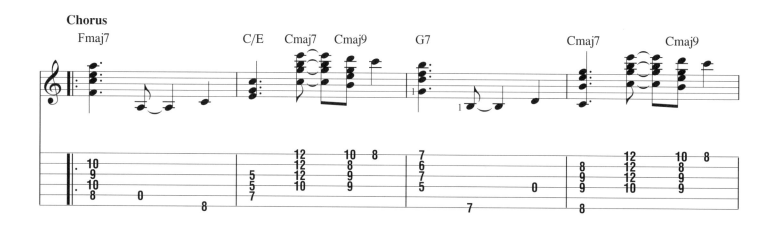

Chorus

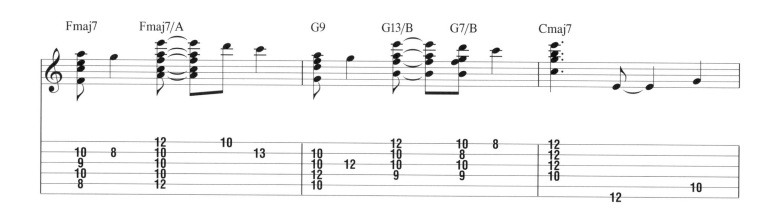

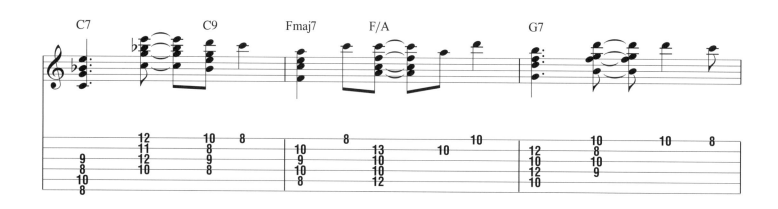

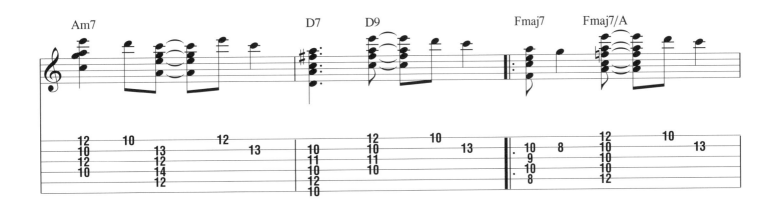

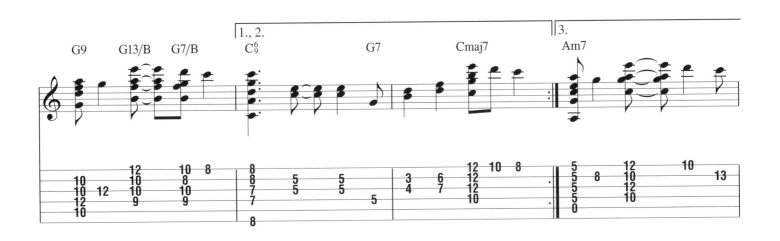

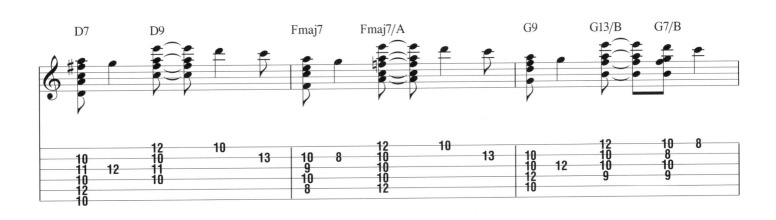

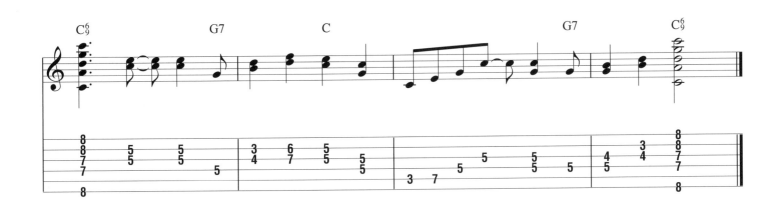

Whistle While You Work

from Walt Disney's SNOW WHITE AND THE SEVEN DWARFS

Words by Larry Morey
Music by Frank Churchill

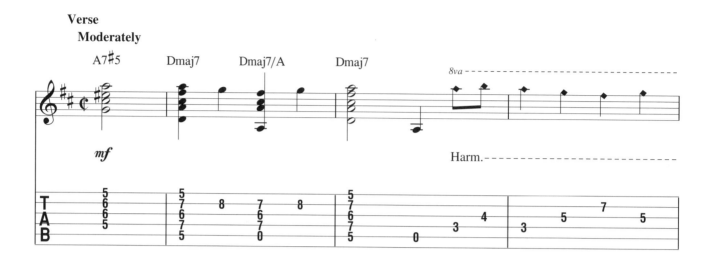

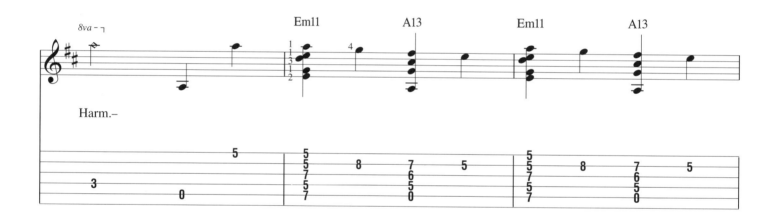

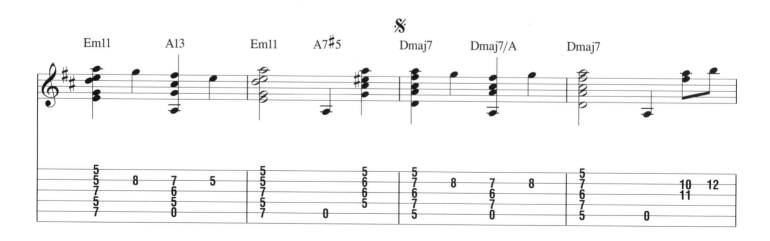

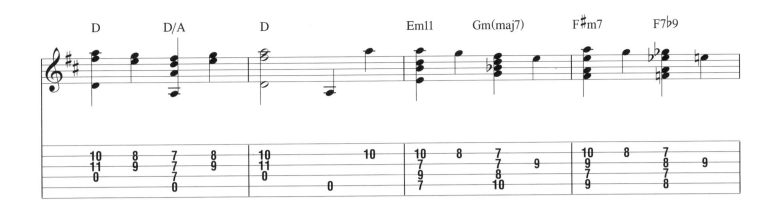

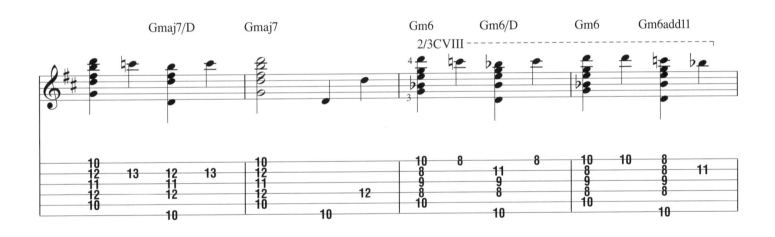

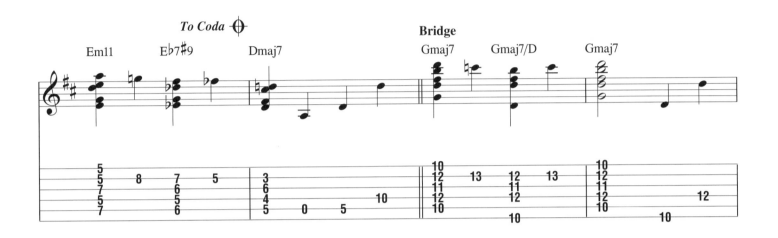

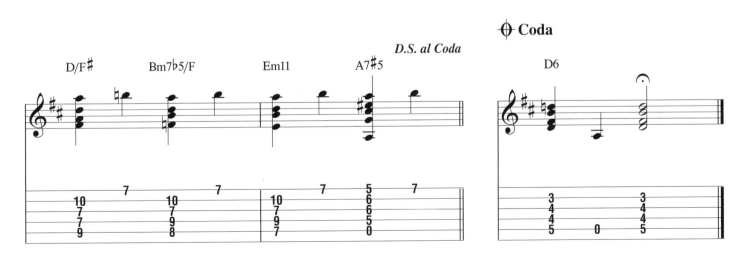

Who's Afraid of the Big Bad Wolf?

from Walt Disney's THREE LITTLE PIGS

Words and Music by Frank Churchill
Additional Lyric by Ann Ronell

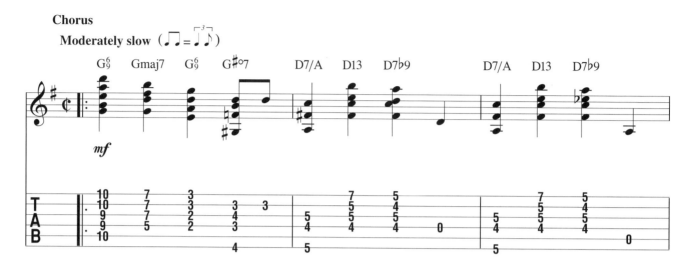

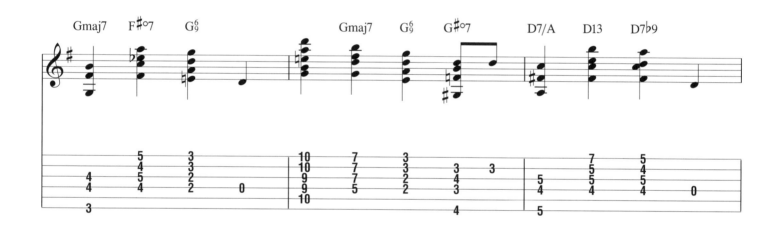

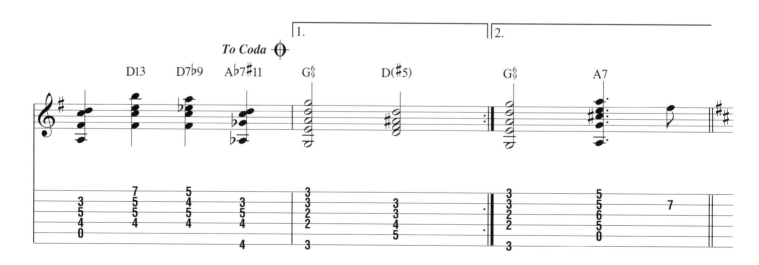

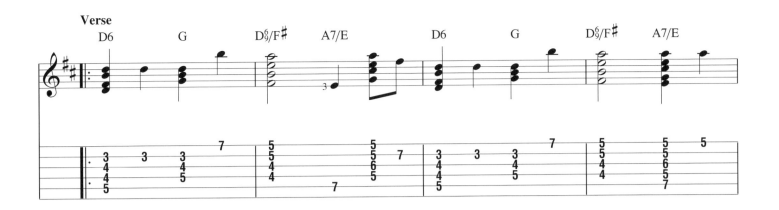

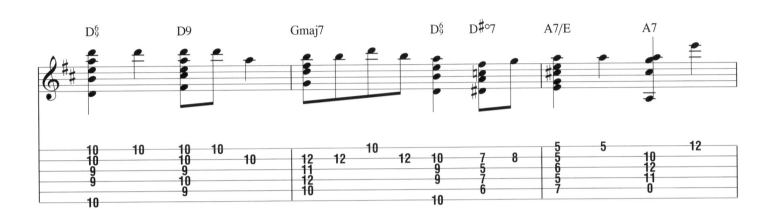

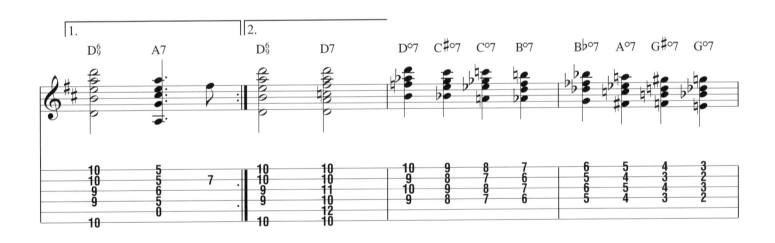

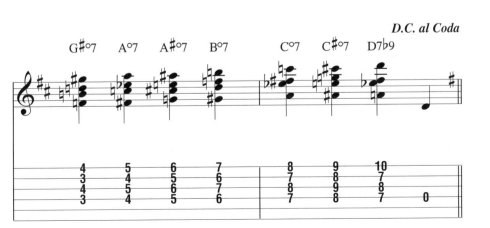

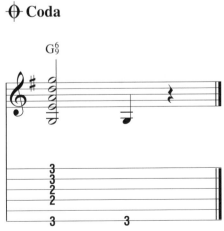

A Whole New World
(Aladdin's Theme)
from Walt Disney's ALADDIN

Music by Alan Menken
Lyrics by Tim Rice

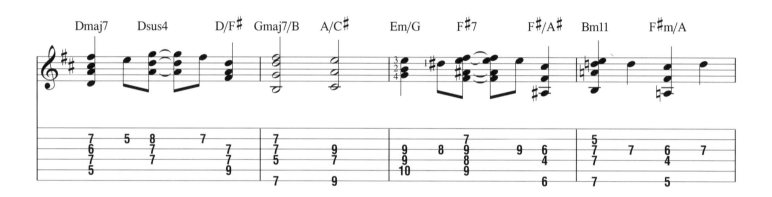

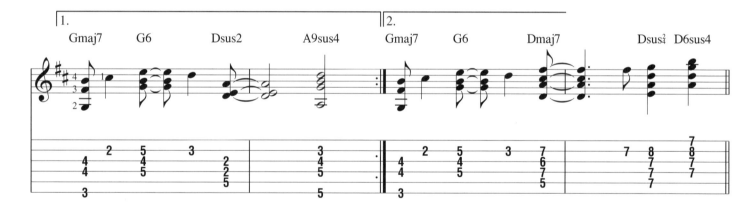

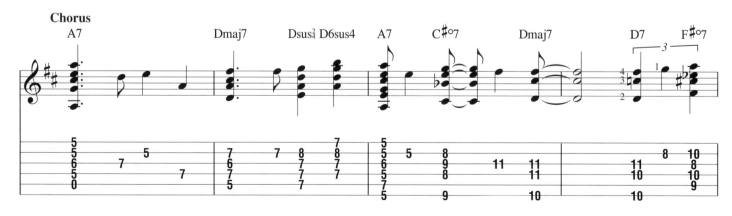

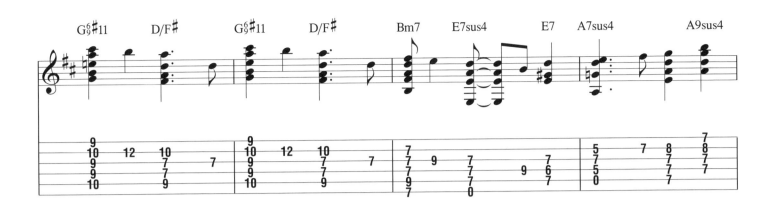

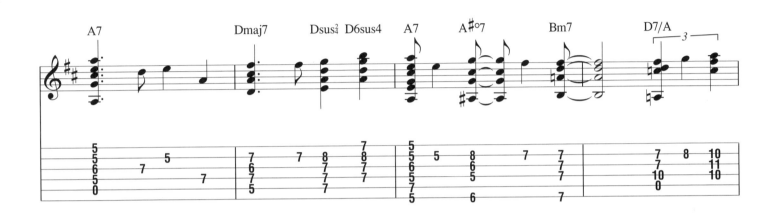

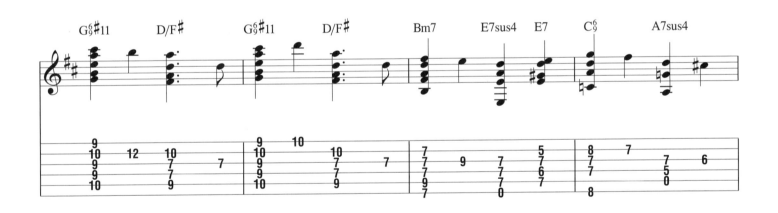

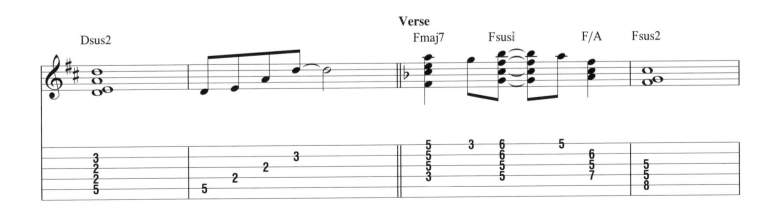

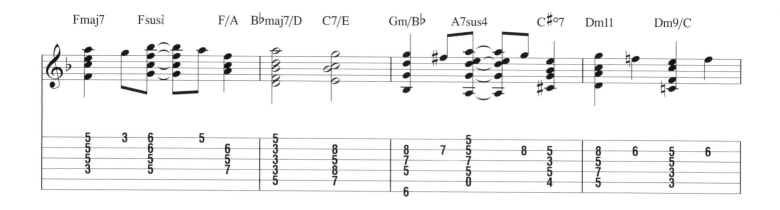

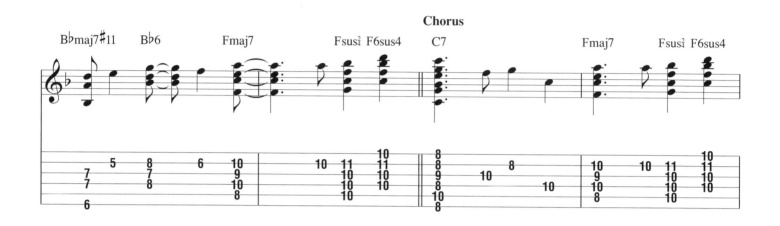

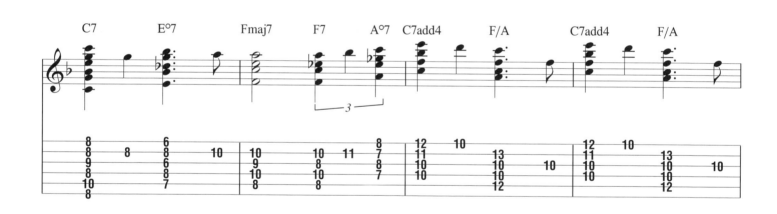

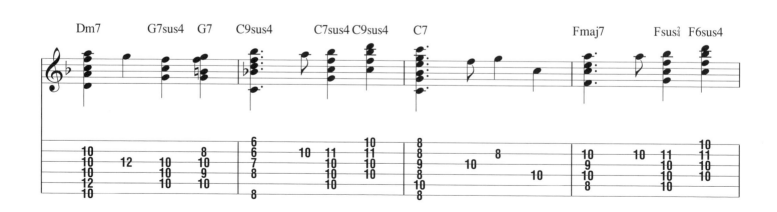

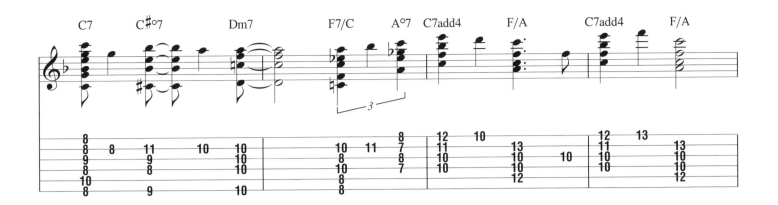

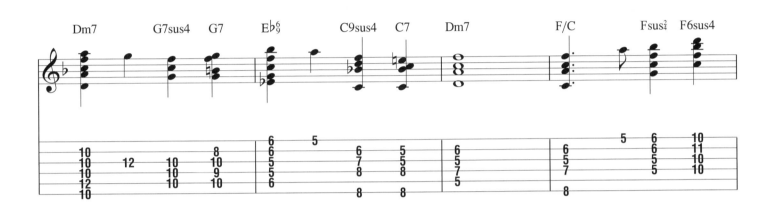

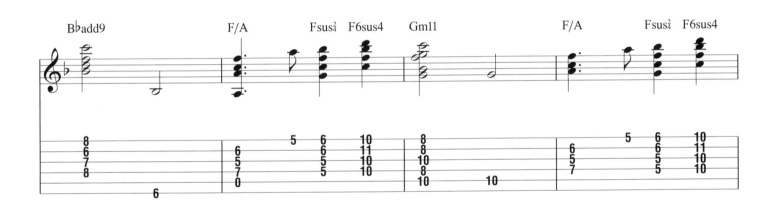

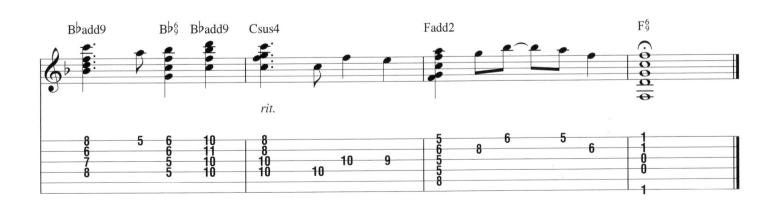

You Can Fly! You Can Fly! You Can Fly!

from Walt Disney's PETER PAN

Words by Sammy Cahn
Music by Sammy Fain

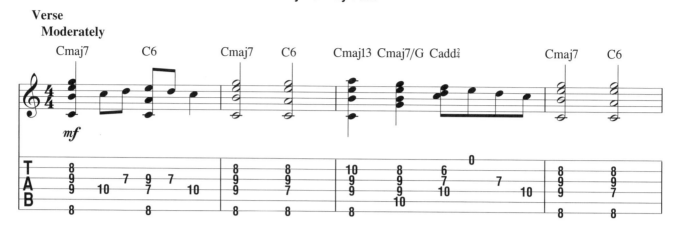

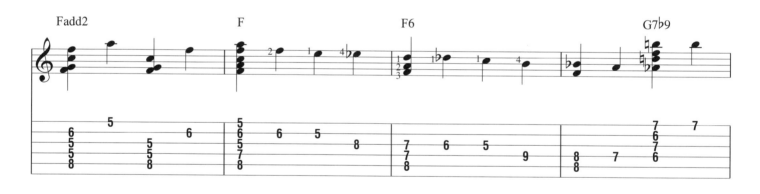

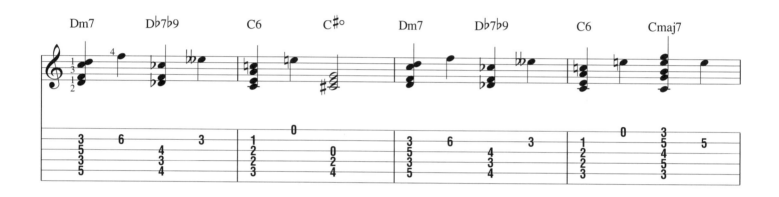

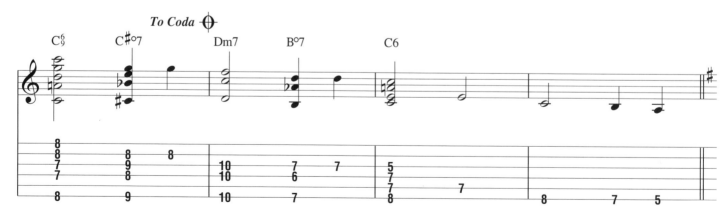

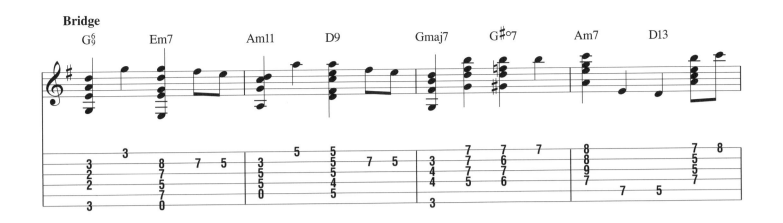

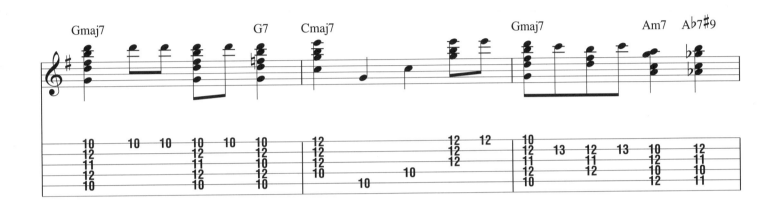

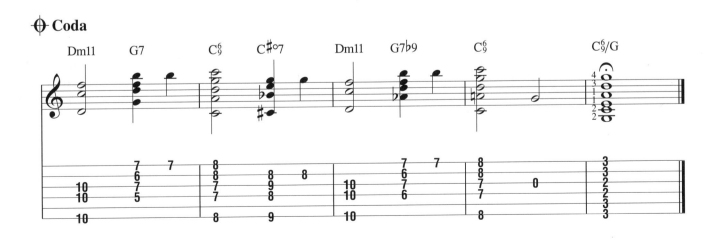

When You Wish Upon a Star

from Walt Disney's PINOCCHIO
Words by Ned Washington
Music by Leigh Harline

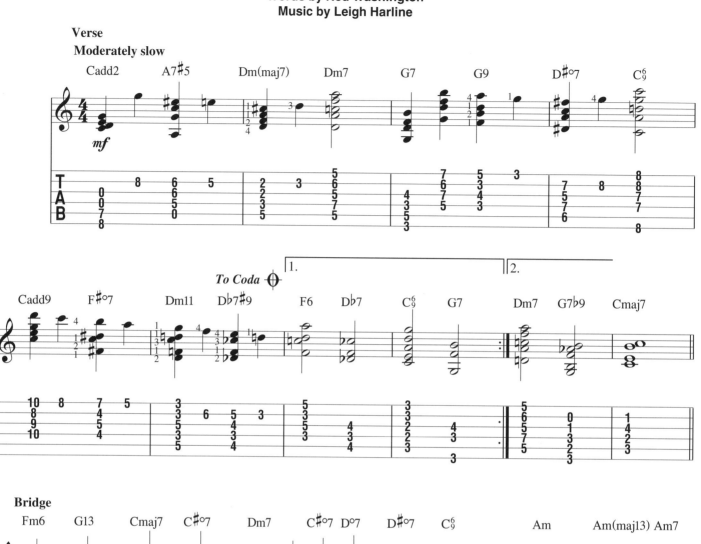

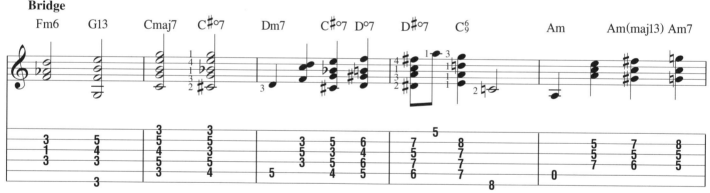

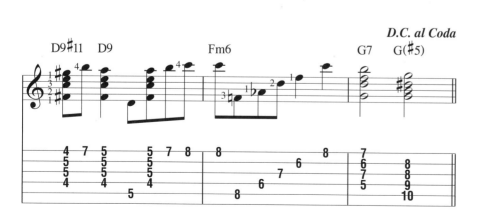

You'll Be in My Heart

(Pop Version)

from Walt Disney Pictures' TARZAN™

Words and Music by Phil Collins

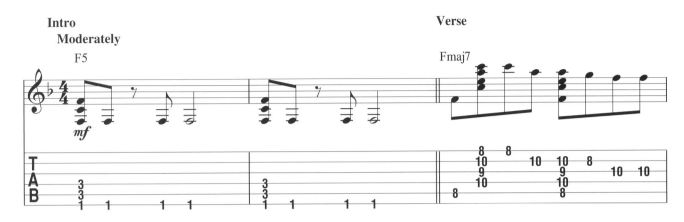

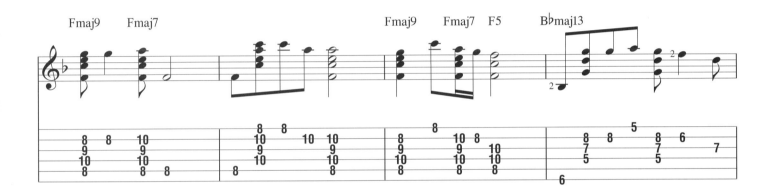

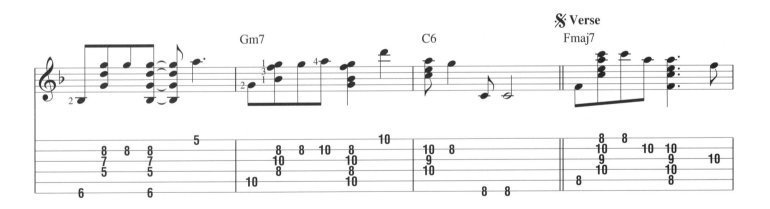

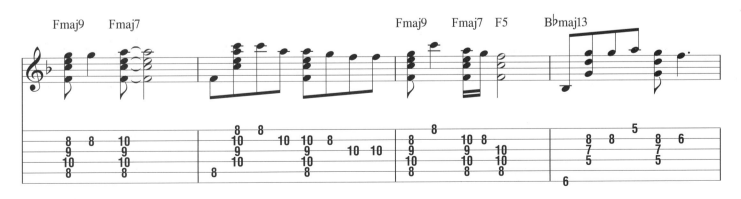

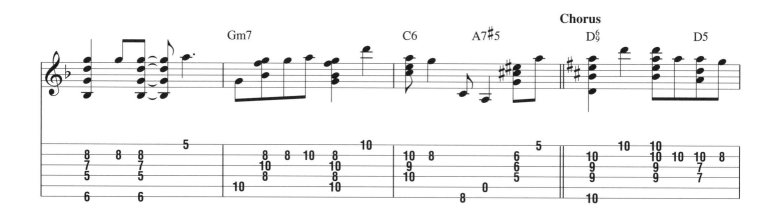

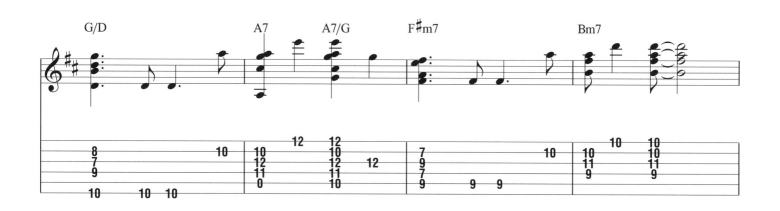

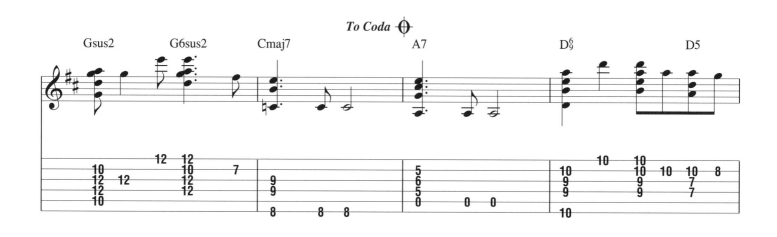

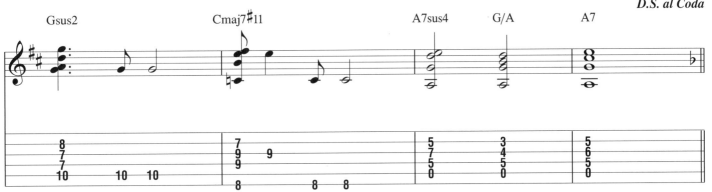

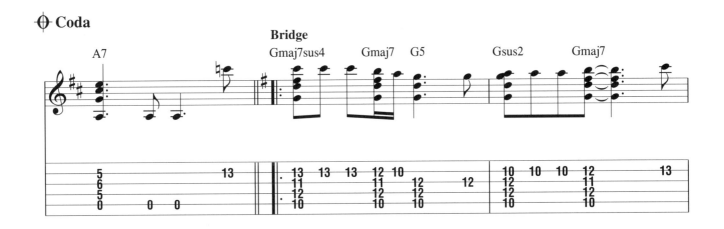

Coda

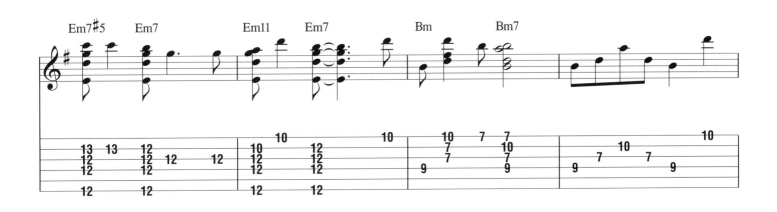

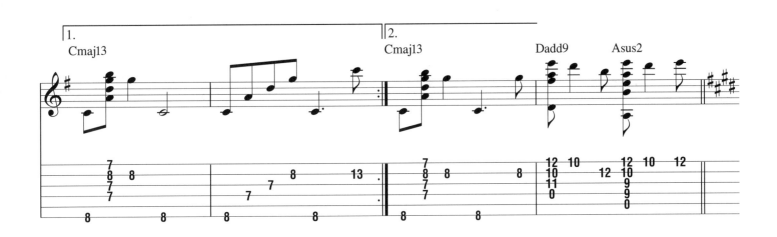

Chorus

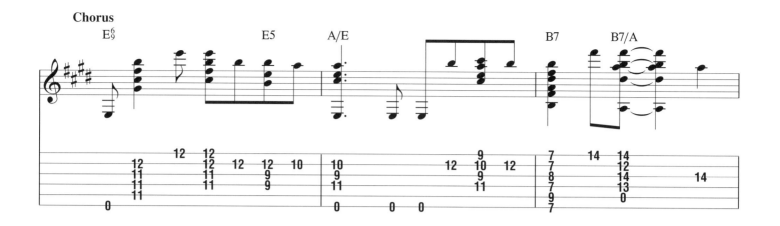

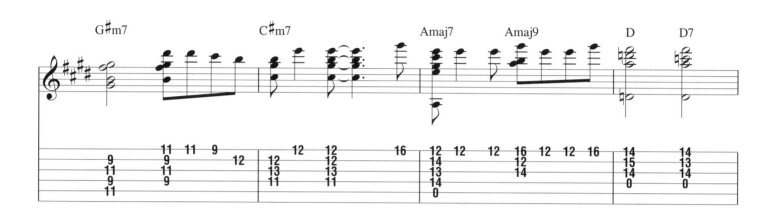

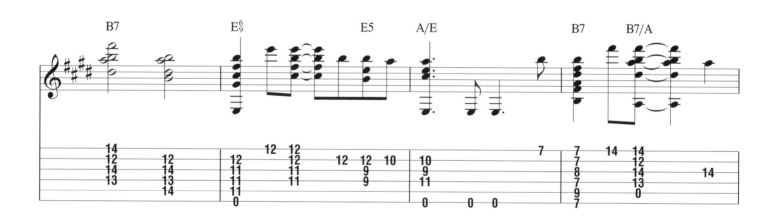

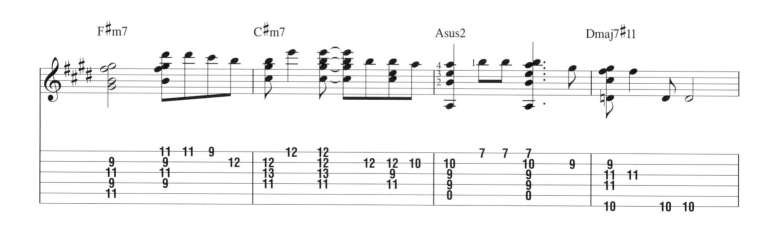

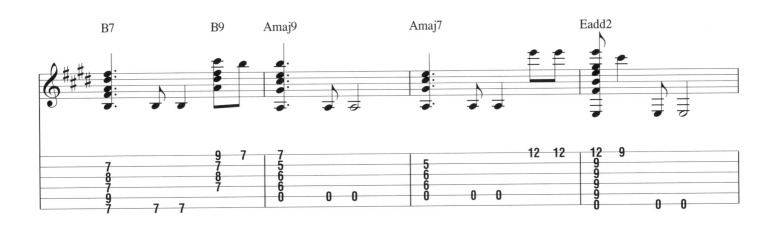

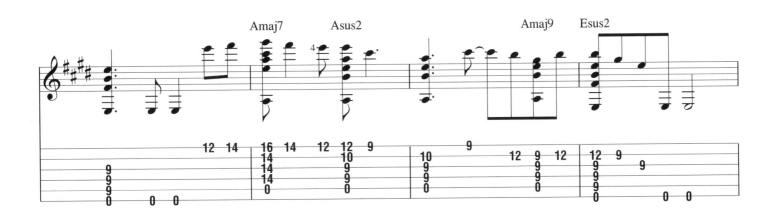

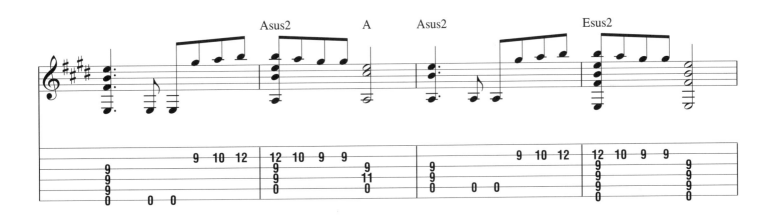

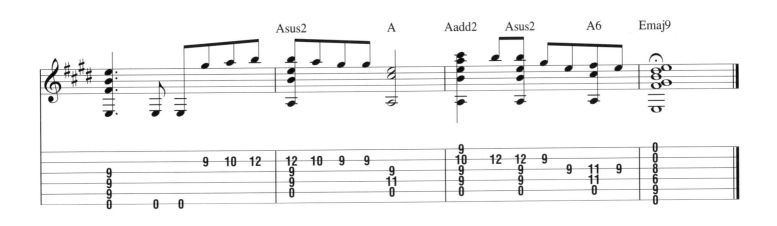

Zip-A-Dee-Doo-Dah

from Walt Disney's SONG OF THE SOUTH

Words by Ray Gilbert
Music by Allie Wrubel

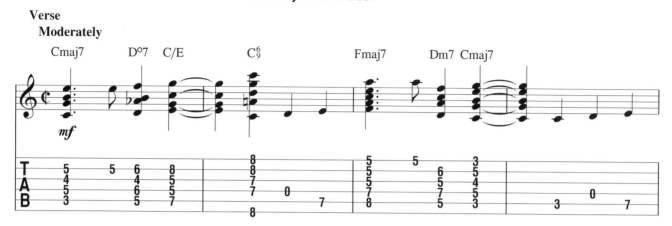

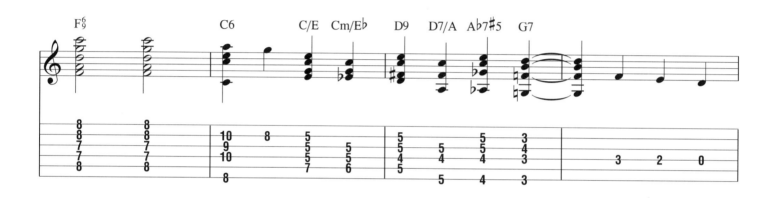

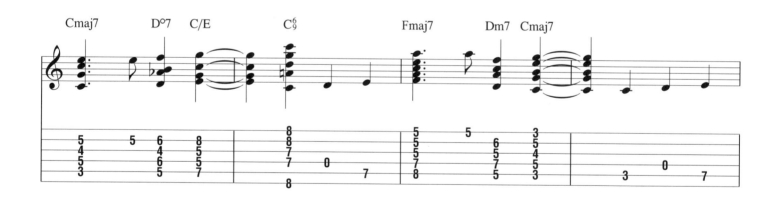

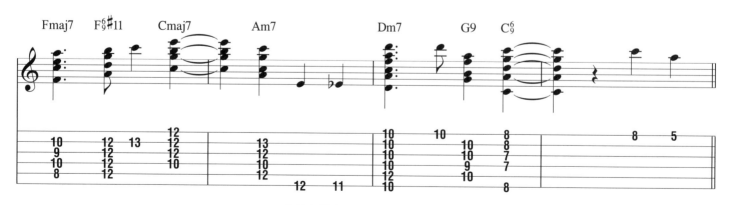

Bridge

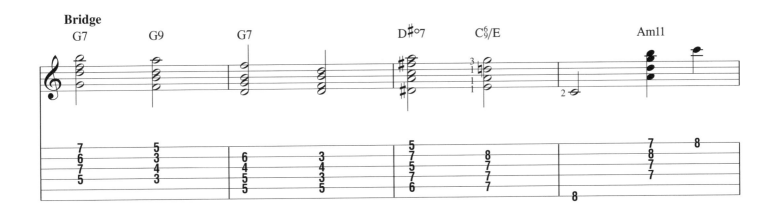

Verse

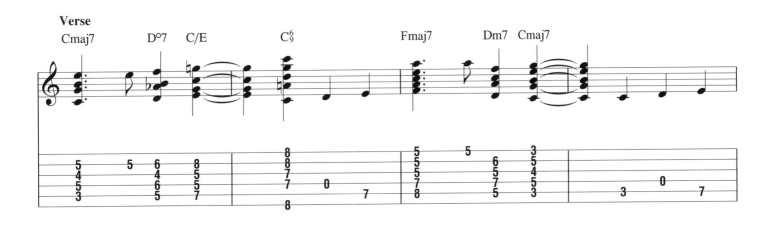

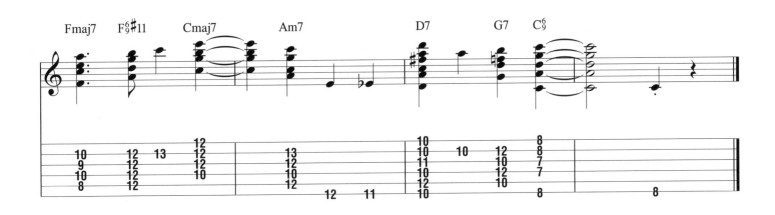